Is This Where We End?

Is This Where We End?

Edited by Oliver D. Kleinschmidt

In collaboration with the
University of Exeter's MA
Publishing Department

This is a work of fiction. Names, characters, places, and incidents either are the product of the author's imagination or are used fictitiously. Any resemblance to actual persons, living or dead, events, or locales is entirely coincidental.

Copyright for this selection and editorial © Little Smiths Press 2023

The copyright of the pieces in this anthology remains with the individual writers. The moral rights of the editor and writers have been asserted.

All rights reserved. No part of this book may be reproduced or used in any manner without written permission of the copyright owner except for the use of quotations in a book review. For more information, address: kleinschmidtoli@gmail.com.

First paperback edition July 2023

Book design by Oliver D. Kleinschmidt

Cover and graphic design by Finley Overland

ISBN 978-1-7391488-5-0 (paperback)

ISBN 978-1-7391488-6-7 (ebook)

Set in Century Old Face

Printed and bound by: IngramSpark

Produced with support from the Department of Creative Writing at the University of Exeter.

Contents

Introduction   i
By The Editor

Her   1
By Nataliia Chubenko

Greening Out   12
By Alexander Masters

Dalliance with a Skin Tag   16
By Amy Rafferty

N-20   23
By Will Moran

Swish   30
By Roberto Oduor

The Train to Retirement   43
By Yulia Zasorenko

Violent Tendencies   50
By Jasmine Collins

The Rules are Different at Sea   61
By Blakeney Clark

Home Is Where the Heart Is   71
By James Albin

The Spectacle   75
By Molly Kirk

Ouroboros   85
By Myles Riley

Everything Ends   100
By Oliver D. Kleinschmidt

Contributors   113

Dedicated to our friends, family, and lovers both past and present. This is for you.

Acknowledgements

We would like to thank all the young writers who were eager and brave enough to have their work edited and formatted for this collection. It is a frightening thing to write a story and see it published so we are grateful to all our writers for their passion to the craft. We would also like to thank the members of the team who helped work on this book, namely Rebeca Bernat for her tireless effort to edit several stories for this collection and to Finely Overland for their constant hard work on the illustrative creative design elements. Another thank you must be extended to the Publishing MA staff at the University of Exeter; without the assistance and teaching of D-M Withers and Davina Quinlivan this book would not exist. One final thanks must go to the dear friends and family who have supported the publication of this book since its inception.

Introduction

By The Editor

No matter who you are or where you go, the chances are you have in some way been involved in a relationship. Now this doesn't necessarily need to be a romantic relationship; in fact, some of my most sincere relationships have been those with my friends and family. As people we are often defined by our relationships with others, and for better or worse the time we spend with the people around us can come to shape how we grow and develop from childhood through to adulthood. With this in mind, it is no wonder that if you asked a cohort of young people in their early twenties to write a short story they would write stories that touch upon the theme of relationships.

When I first conceived of this collection it was initially intended to reflect the anxieties of a younger generation; namely those around climate change and the pervasive use

The Editor

of technology in everyday society. Towards this end I sent out the writing prompt to create a story themed around 'growth' whilst also featuring 'a machine'. Can you guess just what these young, emerging writers would do with that prompt? Unexpectedly, what came back to me were not stories of dystopian futures and cities overgrown with trees but rather, as each new submission came in a pattern emerged.

They were all tied together by themes of relationships.

These were not solely romantic relationships – that would only make things too easy for me – instead I was confronted by an array of stories about parents, friends, guardians, lovers and even work. It became fascinating to see how almost unanimously every young writer submitting chose to write about some sort of relationship that was deep and meaningful to them. Sure enough, as we worked on the stories with each writer it became clear that the stories came from deeply personal places.

Now like many of us when we were infants, I had no real concept of what a healthy relationship could look like. Naturally, I saw the relationships of my parents and my friends, and I watched as all these complex interpersonal dynamics played out between people. It was strange and it was exciting; and as they were developing their relationships with each other I was, unknowingly, also developing my own relationships with them.

The best bonds I've made in this life have been with my family and those select friends I have deemed to be worth

Introduction

having around. It took a lot of time to get there and I'm sure that many of you reading these pages also took a long time to really find a good relationship with the people who you let close to you. I think that is what most relationships truly are, a sense of closeness and comfort in the company of another human being. Although, as you may see through some of these stories, these relationships may not necessarily be with humans. If you take away anything from my little detailed diatribe it's this; the need to feel close to others is key to our relationships and it's simply part of the human experience.

So perhaps that is why, in this time where social media has the power to both bring us closer together and pull us apart our relationships have grown ever more important. Perhaps that is why, when asked to write about 'growth' and 'a machine', people came back with stories featuring important relationships that dispalyed a variety of experiences. If this doesn't show just how much the minds of young people are preocupied with their relationships, then it seems we have much more to learn about how the young mind functions. Relationships are the key cornerstone of society and without them we can find ourselves isolated, alone and feeling increasingly disconnected from those we wish were closest to us. These feelings have only been exasperated in rescent years with the Covid-19 Pandemic only forcing many people to face enforced isolation from thier friends, family and partners.

***

One of the other themes of the initial concept was technology. Whilst the stories do not feature technology too much, I still

The Editor

find the role technology plays on our relationships is incredibly important and isn't something to be condemned but instead embraced. We should work with new media instead of turning away from it. Most young people (namely those of Gen Z), whether they know it or not, have already become enmeshed in this process of change. And who knows what the future may bring, perhaps the next generation of young, emerging writers will write stories with a completely different outlook and approach.

In the following book you will find short stories that are either loosely or directly connected to this core theme of relationships. For relationships are not always obvious, clear, or even particularly well defined between groups and individuals. After all, as we see in *Dalliance with a Skin Tag* a person can fall for something completely inanimate and unresponsive yet still feel deeply, passionately in love. Furthermore, relationships are not purely romantic and some of the earliest and most important relationships in our lives are those we make with our families. But not every family is the same as we see two extremely different families in *Swish* and *Everything Ends*; both divided by tragedy and both dealing with it in entirely unique ways. Throughout each and every story, no matter how subtle, our relationships to ourselves, to those around us and to the very environment we live in are prevalent.

Ultimately, these stories reflect us. Some are very extreme, but they are true reflections of how we can grow and how we feel at different stages of our lives. From childhood through

Introduction

to adulthood and ultimately to our deaths we find our lives intertwined with others and their own lives with their own experiences. If you take anything away after you've read this collection then let it be this; when you can, find someone who you care about, and ask them to tell you something about themselves. Something deep that they've never really told you before. In that small way you'll grow closer, and your relationship with that person will evolve.

Just take a minute, and if you're not alone, look to the people who you've chosen to spend this moment with: are they friends? Is it a lover? A brother or a sister? Are you with a parent? Or are you in the company of strangers? Cherish your relationships and be kind to each other, because as you are about to read, you may never know when it will be your last day on earth.

Her

By Nataliia Chubenko

Track 01. Start Playing

Criminals always come back to the scene of the crime sooner or later.

Always.

I don't remember if someone told me this or whether this was something I simply found on the internet, but this remained as one of those useless facts that you somehow remember a bit too well instead of your lecture material that you'll have on the exam.

I remember that when I heard this saying, I instantly thought that lovers shared a similar trait: that we come back to the crime scene.

The crime scene of a first kiss.

Crime scene of where you two first met.

Nataliia Chubenko

Scene of your first date.

Whatever.

Even if it's just mentally we always come back to it when looking through the darkest corners of our minds.

It's been a long time since I've spent my days wandering around this city, trying to recreate the ghost of someone I couldn't forget. Perhaps, that's why when I decided to return here to visit some of my old friends, I was bold enough to assume that I was able to do this without thinking of Her.

The cruelest thing is that actually, up until that recent snowy night, I was quite successful in that.

***

I was standing at a traffic light, eagerly waiting to cross because of the weather that night.

The wind and the wall of sharp, mean snowflakes stung my skin making my mood even worse. In the low choir of the wind I felt like those damn snowflakes were giggling at how silly I was for forgetting gloves that day. Or maybe it was just my lack of sleep giving me stupid thoughts.

A sigh escaped my chest.

I wasn't enjoying that night. Nor do I ever enjoy nights anymore. I'm too tired.

There used to be a time when I was in love with the heartless charm of nights and when they loved me back. Now, at night, all I feel is the weight of my chronic fatigue resting firmly right under my eyes. Heavy purple bags matching my suffocating necktie.

'Finally.' My grumbling condensed into steam from my mouth when the lights turned green.

I frowned before instantly relaxing my face. My wife said that if I kept frowning most of the time, I'd have even more wrinkles.

I'd already lifted my right foot to cross the traffic light and run down the street back to my hotel when suddenly, the snowflakes giggled at me for the last time, as if not being able to keep in their laughter at the upcoming joke. They appeared to freeze still in the air.

Like curtains in the opera house, the wall of snow parted for a second and I could see the couple across the road.

The snow and the wind silenced, awaiting my reaction...

Track 02. Pause the Song

The first memory of Her appeared to me in the shape and smell of freesias. That and the realization of how no one liked knowing that they weren't the only one.

The danger of a hookup, y'know.

We were both twenty, young, drunk, and still not yet chained by anything. So when the whole thing started, both of us knew it wasn't serious. But even if it wasn't said out loud, we could almost touch the tension flowing in the air between the two of us. She wasn't the only one I was talking to either. Yeah, maybe one night I was ready to give myself to Her but the next day, I knew that I would go back to sending little naughty nothings to others in my DM's too.

I confess, I wasn't a good person in my younger days. Don't mistake me for one.

Still, no matter how bad I was, nobody liked seeing a 'what's up? x' text pop up on the phone of your fuck buddy while the two of you were going home after sneaking past your mutual friends in a club.

And that was when jealousy sparked in the pit of my stomach after seeing that text. I knew I'd completely fucked up.

I almost felt like throwing up. Shouldn't have had vodka cranberry right after a tequila shot.

And shouldn't have been thinking that I was something more to Her than what I actually was.

I remember that night so well.

I wished I looked away faster before seeing that She did pick the phone up.

'Hold on, just gotta tell everyone I left for home.' She said whilst typing. 'Y'know, so they don't search for me.'

'Yeah, sure.'

I wish I didn't want to know who was it that She was actually texting while in a taxi with me. Not like I had the right to complain or like we had a no-texting-other-people-while-we-are-with-each-other rule set. Not like we were the type of people that even followed the rules in the first place.

After all, I still had an unread goodnight text from my girlfriend.

'God, I'm so tired.' I mumbled.

She finally put the phone down and locked the screen.

We passed by the crossroad and for an instant, neon green

light glides against Her skin. Tenderly, slowly, starting from Her face before going down to the jaw line, neck, the low v-cut of Her dress before quickly jumping to Her bare thighs. Even the light was not able to resist clinging to Her skin as if hungrily grabbing the chance to kiss Her for that one short instant.

I knew how it felt, I'd done it myself.

Stealing kisses I had no rights for.

In the library, when I pulled Her away from our studying group to hide in between the shelves.

Every time we ran away from our friends for a 'smoke' break.

On the dance floor, when we could tangle up in the mess of happily drunk bodies.

So, so…so many times in the dark.

Whatever we had between us was so complicated and tangled and wrong, it was a mess of the worst kind, the kind I can't even romanticize and find an excuse for. Yes, I was cheating. Yes, She didn't care. Yes, She was talking to other guys too and I wasn't the only one She fancied.

It was the kind of mess that hurts so good you will later listen to songs that make you re-live that pain again because of how vibrantly alive it makes you feel. But I liked how we were both stuck with whatever we have created between us. Like we were both made so utterly wrong by the universe that our hearts were tailored for each other's hands only. Or so, I felt at that time.

Track 03. Continue Playing

Mere seconds pass as She is crossing the traffic lights accompanied by snowflakes and whoever this man holding Her hand is. Her every step brings Her closer to me and awakens yet another memory of Her.

One.

That's Her asking if I wanted to keep whatever was going on between us a secret. I didn't think much about that request at first so I agreed.

And then spent the entire night overthinking that and wondering how long I had left before She would move on from me.

How long before I forgot what Her freesia perfume smelled like?

Two.

It was a July night. Two days before I was supposed to go back home for the holidays. We were sitting outside, on the porch of my newly rented house, chain smoking and earning our lung cancer.

'What are you thinking about?' Her voice echoed in the dead vacuum of the starry night.

'All the shit I have to pack for the holidays.' I took another drag on my cigarette.

The truth was that I was thinking about how scared I was to break up with my girlfriend and confess my feelings for Her.

My girlfriend was safe. I knew she loved me. I knew she

wasn't going away. I knew she wouldn't choose someone else. Her heart was too pure for a stain like me but I was too scared to leave.

I couldn't bear the 3am cold of my bed sheets. At least not sober. My hands trembled when I thought about ending up alone. I couldn't leave my girlfriend even though I knew that any good person would.

Even if I did leave, I wouldn't be able to be with the one that truly lived in my waking thoughts because with Her, I could never predict anything.

I didn't know if I was worthy of Her. If She would stay with me even if I had done something wrong. If Her heart also felt like it had fallen into a meat grinder every time She didn't get a text from me for an entire day.

But what I did know for certain was that She was speaking to other guys. I knew that She would do what she thought would make Her happy. She was the embodiment of the nights I was in love with; untamed, eyes glittering in the dark, seen for a split second in the dancing crowd. Then you're blinded with neon lights and she's gone to somewhere louder, brighter, warmer. She left when She felt like it was time.

To choose Her felt similar to a leap of faith.

Three.

I stayed up until 4am to talk to Her on the phone because it was the day her father got a call-up paper from the army and Her family did not yet know if he could be dismissed.

I listened to Her talk about it all. About how much She loved her country. About how She did not have any more wishes but for Ukraine to have clear blue skies (She said you need to know what it means yourself). About how there was not a day that She could forget about what was going on. About how She could hear air sirens coming from the phone last time She talked to Her mom.

I let Her talk and talk and talk and I was only thinking about how I wished I was with Her that night and not home, faking being deep asleep.

I remember that night She suddenly asked if I wanted Her to stop talking about it.

'Why?' I asked. 'You can talk to me about anything.'

'Because sometimes when I start talking about it, some people ask me to stop because it's very negative.' I could hear the sarcasm in Her voice. 'For them, it's just negativity. They can ask me not to talk about it or they can scroll past it because it doesn't bother them. But I, and all Ukrainians, still remember that it was Thursday.'

'It was Thursday when what?'

'When it all began.'

I wanted to tell Her that if I could, I would kiss her forehead right there and then and hold her until she fell asleep on my chest. I would let her choose the movie to make her happy and tell her about funny things my dog did that day to distract her from the bad news.

I could show her the playlist I made that reminded me of her to make her feel better.

And if it got really bad and nothing helped, I would stay by her side through all that plagued her mind.

But instead, I only told Her that it was all going to be alright.

Four.

I was sleeping next to my girlfriend and thinking of Her; wondering how much I have sinned in my past life that I got so cursed in this one with just one person.

She has crawled into the darkest pits of my mind.

Amongst all the things worth being afraid of She is the most beautiful one, sitting on a throne; I liked thinking of her in high metaphors.

If she ordered me to I would run to her. Maybe I wanted her to give me an order. Tell me what to do.

Tell me to leave the girl whose love I didn't deserve so she could give it to someone who'd love her the way she deserved.

Tell me to come to Her instead.

I would have done it if She did that. I was too scared to act on my own.

But She never asked anything.

Five.

I remember I got drunk that night. It was just a party with my volleyball teammates.

I hadn't seen Her for quite a while.

Yes, our meetings weren't regular and we could spend a night together and then not see each other for a month but it was the longest I'd gone without seeing Her.

I missed Her.

Not my girlfriend, who was already an ex by then after she'd gotten fed up and left me herself. Her. I missed Her more than I was afraid to admit.

So, I ordered another shot and decided to call Her to tell Her everything.

Track 04. Skip the Song

That was the last time I spoke to her.

In that call, she told me that she started dating someone two weeks ago and she was not going to leave that person. She had made the choice in favor of someone else because She grew tired of waiting for me to make a move.

Someone else to be gentle with Her fears.

To kiss Her forehead. To share his existence with Her.

And I think that's the reason why I could never fully let go of this story. Even after so many years it seems so simple that everything between us could have been different.

It could have been me with Her right now, holding Her hand and crossing the road on a night with an especially nasty wind and heavy snow. I could be the one making Her laugh with the same resonant laughter as when we were twenty. Maybe I could have been the one distracting Her so much that She doesn't even recognize such a familiar stranger. She passes me by while my legs are still chained to the very same spot by the weight of my memories.

The stranger cannot move. She is still laughing and, probably, holding on to the other man's hand tighter as they pass and walk away from me.

She is leaving. And I am still in the same spot, thinking in 'ifs'.

If only I was brave enough.

If only I acted earlier.

If I fixed my mistakes while I had time.

If I broke up with the girlfriend I didn't love.

If only I confessed my feelings to the girl I truly loved while it still mattered.

If, If, If. I can go on with this list forever, but it will not stop the snow from getting more furious around me and the wind from giggling into my ears at my helplessness.

Nor will it stop Her, walking away from me with someone who was not afraid to confess first.

I saw Her.

Taking away my heart with Her.

And leaving nothing behind but the smell of freesia.

Greening Out

By Alexander Masters

Will sat on a disgusting green couch that bent to fit the corner. He was deep in a k-hole; the keys he'd snorted off were still dusted with ketamine. He was taking long, deep breaths, like he was about to go diving. Finn's eyes were fixed to a spot on his forehead.

Will...

Yeah? He squeaked between white lips.

What you doing man?

I can't swim this deep!

What?

I'm fucking drowning, Finn!

'We're in the kitchen mate.'

'Oh, right yeah.' He sucked in another massive lungful of air. His leg kicked out involuntarily and he looked on the verge of tears. I couldn't help but watch.

'...Finn?' He passed a hand over his face like he was wiping water from his eyes.

'I'm right here.' He said.

'It's too deep, I'm gonna drown!'

'You're still in the kitchen.'

'Oh my god!' Will moaned, slumping even deeper into the sofa.

Julia giggled, her head leaden as she threw it back against the windowsill behind her. She looked up, her eyes catching the light like marbles, yellow cataracts burning in her pupils. She looked the tiniest bit more aware than I felt. She was pretty, with curly blonde hair and soft, rounded features. Her collarbones stood out from her skin, and her eyes bore into everything she stared at. There was always a predatory look on her face, like a shark.

How did I end up here? In a disgusting kitchen on a rank sofa. Someone was trying to grow a new species of mold in a collection of dirty dishes left on the table.

A year ago, the night before my eighteenth birthday, I'd drunk a cider at a concert ... and spent the next morning bent over a toilet swearing to God that I'd never drink again.

That night I went out again; the same experience awaited me when I got back home. It was worse than the one before and I pulled my back muscles from retching. To cut a long story short, I don't have the enzymes to metabolise the toxins in alcohol; in other words, I'm allergic. I'd pondered how I was going to make it through uni. It was going to be hard to have a social life when most students based theirs around a drinking culture interwoven with early mornings and bad sex. Or at least, that's what I'd seen. Clubs were about as fun as headbutting concrete when you were sober, and you just look like a prick stood at the bar with lemonade. I resented being cut off from everyone else, even in such a trivial way.

My solution came to me in the form of Khan. He was tall, skinny, and always wearing a slightly worn oversized hoodie. In fact, after all the times I saw him I don't remember ever having seen him not wearing it. A few weeks before I moved away, I bumped into him at a party and we started talking. He was pretty rough, and he made me nervous, but I shrugged it off and tried to look tough. Twenty minutes into us talking he pulled a kitchen knife from his waistband to show me how tough he was, so I guess that didn't work. Anyway, after a few awkward messages of me trying to work out what the measurements meant, I finally got high for the first time. No retching, no throwing up, not even a headache. Salvation.

***

Julia held out happiness in vapour form, and I took a drag on the embers pinched between my fingers. Smoke burned the back of my throat, drying it instantly and making my eyes water. I held my breath for a few seconds, then released the smoke gently before letting it gather about my head like a veil. It curled back towards my face as I breathed in through my nostrils, tendrils creeping at the inside of my skull. I passed the joint to Julia, whose eyes were turning bloodshot. They were fixed on me, shining still. Will hooted, his eyes rolling to the back of his head. He fell silent and still, and Finn's eyes never left one spot on Will's forehead.

We passed the spliff back and forth until the lit end scorched my fingers. I leant towards the table and mashed it out in someone's bowl; a petri dish that had grown fur to properly insulate weeks old bolognaise.

I leaned back, melting into the sofa. My arms and head were lead weights but my entire body felt light enough to float. Julia slid up the couch next to me and leaned against me. I couldn't even turn my head. She giggled and her head slipped to my neck, resting her cheek against my collarbone. I wanted to tip my head the other way but I felt as though my bones were melting, and the strength flowed from my body, forced out through my veins by an unyielding heartbeat. Her face stayed where it was, laughing, as she swung a fish-netted leg over mine. She'd straddled me, pining me against the sofa, another lead weight adding to the hundreds I already felt. She was crushing me, her weight pressing down on my hips, my legs going fuzzy and static. Her hands gripped either side of my face, semi-cupping my cheeks. She leant down and kissed me, her blonde curls obscuring the room. I could barely move my lips; I was so stupidly high. Panic flooded through me, and I tried to tighten the muscles in my neck but I had nothing left.

I opened my mouth to speak but no sound came out, and it only gave her room to slip her tongue inside. I was being smothered, as though she were melting into me rather than just on top. I felt like bile was rising in my throat, a surge of nausea sending waves around my skull. I tried to turn my head but couldn't. So I lay limp, turning the same shade of green as the sofa.

Dalliance with a Skin Tag

By Amy Rafferty

When I first met my husband at the tombola after mass, his opinions on the human body unnerved me. Later, over a bottle of merlot, he explained to me how the corporeal body is an indifferent machine.

'Essentially Gladys, the body is an ideal witness to human atrocity. An objective and impartial spectator to the cycles of life and death it accommodates. Neutral and unloaded, its ethics remain unclear. The body cannot speak and cannot truly feel. It can only sense and produce physiological responses to material stimuli.'

I sat there intoxicated and uncomfortable, impregnated with the communion I'd consumed that morning. The flesh and blood in my stomach swelled at the inadequacies of his corporeal creed. It was at that moment, that my body itself responded, the merlot splattered across the carpet: along with rice, carrots, and a tense shift in atmosphere.

He was wrong. He had omitted essential counterpoints to his argument. The aching desires, combustible urges, spasms both voluntary or otherwise. His entire philosophy and smug sneer could be undermined by his dismissal of the stimuli that comes from within.

Our marriage and life together began as a mission, to go forth and multiply, spread the good word, and share loaves with sinners. However, ten years in with no baby and dwindling church attendance, I suspect my husband's faith to be repossessed by the scientific principles of his bodily beliefs. In an attempt to reconnect, I have adopted an empirical mindset, conducting experiments and collating data to disprove his initial thesis. Thus far, my study has proven unfruitful and I fear his ideological chemistry will remain unchained. Nevertheless, I have discovered recently that his own conduct and creation disprove his phlegmatic credo.

Ever since I found them at the bottom of the garden, and moved us to Westerly Point, I've been seeing a lot more of his back. Not that I'm offended. For without my husband's shunning, I never would've met Him. One night, dangling on the precipice of sleep, I met Him. Jutting out towards me, his presence inescapable. He is like nothing I have ever seen before. Knobbly and misshapen, discoloured and grey in some parts, plump and vibrant in others. His hairs are wispy and thin, curling beautifully at the ends.

Of course, I'm not talking about another man, but the rhubarb growth on my husband's back. God, he is beautiful. He never speaks, wanting me to do all the talking. I happily and eagerly oblige. I have so much to say. My husband refuses to listen to me. Not after the garden incident. Previously he indulged me, but the exposure of his secret has established an impassable gulf between us. I have found a means to fill this gulf. I have found Him.

I never thought a love like this was possible. My sentiments have manifested in a creation that feels dictated by God and my husband's body alone. For the first time I feel seen, not just observed. In this new nocturnal relationship: I am not told what to wear, how to eat, my body is not prodded and poked, I am not made fun of at the dinner table to entertain the guests. The gristly Galatea to my Pygmalion would never burn long awaited Christmas cards from church friends before I've read them.

I remember the grainy warts that adorned my father's sagging lobes at the breakfast table. The unswallowable cereal mulch sat at the back of my throat. But he is different. My father's malign ornaments were dead, laden with puss and infection. I know He is alive. I can sense the throbbing vessels inside Him synchronising with my own quickened heartbeat. He just hangs on my husband's back and listens to my outpourings. If He could, I know He would reach out and embrace me. But the comfort and love He provides is more than enough.

In his disgust and contempt, my husband's body has produced for me a capillary filled companion of love and acceptance. A fleshy reward for my pleas and woes. His innards are exposed, pushed outwards to face me. Despite his repulsion towards me, his body has deviated from programming and treated me with this freckled gift. I have never been more satiated and content. Dormant and innate feelings have been stirred once more, alongside sensations of a new and intense calibre. As I stare at him tonight, I am charged. I am full of raw feelings. I am the anomaly. I must cross my legs to contain myself.

Dalliance with a Skin Tag

My growth of a gigolo is enticing to say the least. I entertain Him with my hot breath, indulge myself with tentative prods and pokes when my husband is raptured in deep slumber. It is in these twilight hours that I bring my lover gifts of ice cubes, ointments and talc. My smooth digit caressing His rough and scaly peel is an overwhelming sensation muffled only by pillows and cool linen bed sheets. I create situations that bring us together whenever possible. I buy my husband shirts of sheer materials so that the protrusion can be observed in daylight, His glorious colourings exposed. I turn the thermostat up at night so that my husband overheats and takes his vest off and my amorous angioma reveals itself. I waste away days, praying for the lights of the skies to drain away to dusk. I sit in my arm chair, picking at my nail beds until they bleed, waiting for the time we can retire to bed.

And so here we are in bed, staring at each other on the eve of our parting. I can't allow it, I won't. He brings me more peace than lying dead in a still river's reeds or staying the night in the womb. Without Him I sit in constant purgatory waiting for my husband's eyes of judgement to peer over the *Daily Times*. When I lie with Him, I know I did the right thing. When I cry in front of my soft and sweaty growth, I cry with Him. My tears are not met with anger and outrage, they are amiably received. I don't feel ashamed or embarrassed, simply comforted by this silent and swelling red mass. There is a pickling jar and a scalpel in my bedside table. My tools, ready to carve away my love. I swiped the blade from the nursing station at the hospital the day we said goodbye to the babies. I refused to leave empty handed and was desperate to join my taken angels that night.

It's strange, unable to produce and love the growths of my own body, I have become connected to that of my husband. I believe I am raptured by my beloved because of His ability to constantly change and grow. I am raptured with amorous pride when I witness His pulsating progress. My husband despises the natal nevus however, sentencing my paramour to removal and incineration. My new love is perceived by my husband to be a fleshy reminder of the impossible standards of restriction set for him by both the world and himself. An outward ugliness for his inner decay. The beautiful blot on my husband's fleshy canvas is a nuisance, an itchy and weeping blemish that disrupts his sleek unwavering visage.

My husband has been branded with a mother's mark of eternal epidermal judgement; the sole kindness his body has ever given me. I wonder if his mother knows about his appetites? Perhaps it explains her aversion to the wedding and the balls of yarn for baby clothes left regrettably untouched.

I will also take my jewels with me, and my mother's rosary beads are in my pocket. We leave tonight. I lace my husband's whisky with sleeping pills at dinner, so he will remain unaware of our escape. I've prepared this cocktail for him once before, after John scuttled home and my husband felt homicidal.

My lover waits. Sometimes hot, sometimes cold, sometimes sweaty, sometimes dry. Forever gorgeous and beautiful. I cannot live without Him. Perhaps we shall retire to the country, or Paris, or somewhere near the water. There are so many things I want to show him: the hospital, the church, the graves, maybe even the old house with its periwinkle bathroom and creaky steps. The barren nursery.

I miss the garden so much. But it is tainted now. Weeds strangle my garden ornaments, left orphaned and exposed in the wake of our suburban exodus. The pond is stagnant and reeks. Events of that day have turned my Eden stale and overgrown, a place I cannot return to.

Outside the hangnail moon is waning, but my desires are burgeoning. The ceremonial tools are organised beside me on the pocket spring altar. If I start the operation on the hour, we'll be out of the house by quarter to. Restricting myself before, for fear my husband would wake up, I start to explore Him with my other senses. I lick Him ever so slightly, his bumps grazing my smooth wet tongue. There's logic to my actions. Lubrication will make removal an easier and swifter process.

The flesh on my husband's back is easy to penetrate, like slicing into a fatty sponge. I can feel myself oscillating between anger and gratitude as his blood soaks my fingertips. This is all his doing. I have never had anything just for myself, I have always had to share. My school shoes arrived scuffed and stretched. The one cup of the thermos we brought on walks belonged to him. In the confessional, my time with the Holy Father was always interrupted by the priest. My paradise was cohabited. I was expected to live in the shadows when his associates came over at the weekends, emerging only when his violence required an outlet. The flowers I planted hadn't served me, only provided a colourful leafy backdrop for our marital lapse. An associate of my husband had come up from London for lunch. I found them trampling on the delicate buds, crushing the silken petals under the weight of their amorous embraces. I went back inside and prepared lunch.

I feel the scalpel snag as I attempt to go further but cease redress, as my love is now detached, a pink plump nub in the palm of my hand. Delicately I place Him in the jar and get out of bed. I place the bloody scalpel in my pocket alongside the rosary and leave the bedroom. I put on my coat and leave through the front door, posting my keys back through the letter box. My smile cannot leave me, I am just so happy, so relieved. My circumstance is isolated and special, scientific conclusions cannot be drawn as much as moral ones can.

Perhaps one day, with adequate love and nature, my paramour will grow. Perhaps arms will emerge, even teeth and lips. If His hair grows coarser, I shall brush and braid it. I request that my lover fails to develop a voice and remains silent; it really is one of the metiers of our dynamic.

Finally, we are alone together. I peak into the jar and see condensation forming on the sides. I clutch the jar close to my chest and head into the night, craving a glass of merlot.

My husband won't be too upset I have left, taking with me the part of him I love most. For my new jarred lover was nothing but a nuisance for him, an irritating itch in the centre of his back impossible to access by hand. I have done him a favour. Besides, he is now free to fill my dip in the mattress. Perhaps he will invite John up from the city. I hope too that his appetites are satiated when I leave. Perhaps over coffee and a grope of the neighbouring thigh he will realise that the body's position as ideal witness derives from its inability to be impartial. My experiment will reach a satisfying conclusion. I will win this fight.

N-20

By Will Moran

The coffee shop of the 9/11 Memorial Museum sat on a mezzanine overlooking the main floor, separated from it by a Perspex screen. Amelia sat with her knees tucked under her chin, leaning her cheek against the Perspex, and listening to the buzz all around her. She tried to hear the museum far below – the audio recordings, the newscasts, the sounds of performative grief – but it was all absorbed by the Perspex and replaced with easy chatter. *How's the doughnut? Should we check out the Met after this?*

She took a sip from her water bottle, paying attention to it moving down her throat. Her chest felt heavy, a boulder in the place of her heart. There was meant to be something else – sadness, grief, guilt – any kind of feeling that would attach her to this moment. But there was nothing but the rock, and she imagined the water swelling around it, failing to move forward.

Colin approached her, darting through the web of plastic chairs, and she straightened up.

'I brought you a cup of tea,' he said when he reached her. 'I couldn't remember how you take it so I left it black. But there's packets of milk over there if you want some.'

He waited for a reply and, when none came, set the Styrofoam cup down in front of her and pulled out his chair. She winced as the legs scraped the pine floor.

As she placed her feet on the ground, Colin sipped his coffee and sneered at the bitterness. The steam from her cup tickled her face for a moment before she took a sip. It was awful.

'Where have you been?' she asked, the words sticking in her throat. 'We finished in the Family Room at least half an hour ago.'

'I went through the main section,' he replied, and when she said nothing continued, 'would you like to go?'

'No.' The dead air hung between them. She took another sip.

'I shouldn't have asked that.'

'But you did.'

He drummed his knee under the table until her tea began to spill on the plastic-coated tablecloth. She swirled the droplets with a finger, making a tic-tac-toe board.

'Where's your mum?' he tried again.

'She's in the archive, looking for a watch she bought him that she wants to give to Jack.' She drew an X in the centre of her makeshift board. 'And one of his leg-bones is in there.'

She met Colin's eyes and he shifted uncomfortably.

'Ah.' he ducked his head to take another sip of coffee. 'Okay.'

The rock pressed down in her chest and wave of disgust followed. She began to tap her fingers on the table, taking pride in the annoyance building on his face.

'We don't belong here,' she said.

'What do you mean?' he kept his tone even.

'Well, you wouldn't be here if she wasn't your wife. And I wouldn't be here if she wasn't my mum.'

His eyes softened with pity. 'He was your dad.'

'You don't have to tell me that when you know I don't believe it. And I know you don't either.'

He reached across and stopped her shaking hands. Her nails felt crushed inside his calloused palms, and she fought the urge to wrench them away. After all, he was trying. But the rock wouldn't budge.

'I wouldn't be here if she wasn't my wife, no,' he said, gentle and slow. 'I don't feel grief right now, no. But I can be here for her. I can connect to it through her. And if that's what you need to do for now, look at it like that.'

Now that she had his gaze, she found she couldn't take the force of it, so she closed her eyes and focused on the noises around her once more. The coffee machine stood out to her, its whirring and hissing steam. It occurred to her that they were all gathered in this room because that machine was here and without it, they could be anywhere else. But if it disappeared right now, she and Colin and all these people would be sitting here with a void where the central point of meaning should have been.

Tears began to leak from her eyes.

'She wants me to feel it for me. I don't know how.'

He squeezed her hands. 'You will, one day. And until then, try your best.'

'It's too much.' There was too much those words could mean.

'I know. But one day it won't be.'

'When?' her voice was thick with tears now, her face reddening with the effort of appearing calm. 'How do you know?'

'He was your dad.'

Colin wrapped her fingers around the rapidly cooling Styrofoam and let go, moving to sit back. He seemed satisfied with himself and got his phone out of his pocket to check messages.

She watched him coolly for a few moments, then scraped her chair back as loudly as she could, reached for her tea and slammed it into the table. Scorching droplets speckled her wrists and the cuffs of Colin's shirt. As she bolted for the lift, he didn't try to follow.

**

Outside, the sun stung her eyes. It had been misty when they'd arrived, and too early for most tourists. Now, as it approached noon, the courtyard around the memorial pools was packed. Searing light reflected from the thousands of phone screens and her eyes darted frantically as she looked for a safe place to hide.

Then she realised why there were so many phones out. Most of the tourists weren't taking pictures of the museum or its surroudings. Most were taking selfies with beaming smiles. Some pushed themselves up onto the engraved memorial stones and sat, posing.

Bile rose in her throat. She tried to remember that for most people this place was a tourist attraction. They had to be reminded to 'never forget'. When they got home the pictures might make them stop and pause, but more likely they would be swiped over in favour of the Statue of Liberty. They were just people. People don't always think.

But she couldn't. She hated them. She hated every single beaming smile. Her brain felt like it was breaking in two – in one plane of her mind, she reached for the couple sitting cross-legged on the polished stones and tore them off and screamed *read their names* to tell them they were crushing someone, that person was nothing but ash that had been collected into plastic bags and given out at random and the families had had to hope that some of that ash was the person they loved and those families didn't have anywhere else to go, this is it, this is the place we can come to remember and can't you –

In the real world, she only ran until she found a quiet spot, her vision bleached white from the sun, her chest and throat pounding.

When the sounds of people quieted, she stopped and took a few minutes to breathe, focusing only on the water in the memorial pools. Its rush like a guided meditation. Slowly, she blinked until the spots in her vision cleared and looked around.

She had run to the top-left corner of the North Memorial,

away from the entrance. There was a man with a backpack a short way from her with his head bowed, silent. She felt an unexpectedly powerful urge to hug him.

Instead, she looked down at the dark stones and found the designation in the bottom-left corner. N-20.

Her stomach sank into the deep recess of the pool as she searched the stone carefully. *There*. It was him that she'd run to.

The rock in her chest shattered.

Sobs wracked through her body like the water in her ears had entered her head and was flooding out from wherever it could. She reached her hand out and placed it on his name to steady her and the waves rushed through her, stronger and stronger. But she didn't let go. She wouldn't leave him.

Eventually, she ran dry. The skin over her forehead and under her eyes was tight and raw. Her head was fuzzy, her throat dry. Yet she felt cleared, having burned like a forest, right down to the roots.

Her back pocket buzzed and she pulled out her phone. It was a text from Mum.

'Finished at archives. Sorry it took so long, honey. Are you still at café? Xx.'

'I'm outside,' she replied.

The three grey dots appeared for longer than they needed to. She imagined Colin telling her about the outburst, her not knowing what to say to either of them.

'With him?' It came through.

'*Yes.*'

She could almost feel the shock of that reply. Mum's fingers hovering over the phone, trying not to ruin it. The same tears welling in twinned eyes.

'*Stay there as long as you need. I'll come find you when you're ready.*'

Swish

By Roberto Oduor

Monday, July 17th - 8:00 AM

'BZZT. BZZT. BZZT. BZZT.'

Rosie groans as she stretches out her arm and gropes around the floor to find her phone. She seizes the offending device and quickly turns off the alarm. The monotonous mechanical melody ceases, and Rosie switches off before her phone does.

Monday, July 24th - 8:00 AM

'BZZT. BZZT. BZZT.'

'Five more minutes...' Rosie reasons sleepily; grabbing her phone from her nightstand.

As she's about to tap the 'Snooze' button, she checks the time, her eyes half-open.

'8:00. Game time!' The phone reads.

'Urgh-why?' She complains mentally. Tentatively, she pokes her foot out from her covers.

'I've got the whole day ahead of me,' she thinks, sliding her foot back into the warmth of her sheets. Half-dazed, she remembers how quickly the bedding used to be yanked off her mattress last summer. She wraps her face with her duvet to block out the memory.

Wednesday, July 26th - 8:30 AM

'BZZT.BZZT.'

Rosie's left hand automatically reaches for the phone, but it's not on her nightstand. She raises her head; her brain failing to register the continued buzzing.

Blinking fervently, she makes out a blue hue in the opposite corner of her room.

With a sigh of resignation, Rosie reluctantly withdraws from the cocoon of her bed covers.

The hairs on her forearms automatically rise in response to the morning air.

'Why is it so cold?' Rosie complains.

Wednesday, July 26th - 11:45 AM

Rosie wipes sweat from her forehead, panting heavily. Two feet away, a lone basketball rests on the driveway, untouched.

The bushes and the birch tree branches swish and sway in the cool summer breeze. Rosie glances upwards, her face contorted in discomfort.

'Maybe just one more set of sprints,' she muses.

As if in response, a mild spasm shoots through her leg and back.

'OK, OK! You win,' she concedes.

Rosie limps into the kitchen. The sound of boiling water, accompanied by a slight burnt smell fills the room. Rosie swipes a tumbler from the countertop and heads towards the fridge.

'Whoa!' Rosie's father exclaims, turning away from the stove to face her as she grabs a large soda bottle from the fridge. 'How long were you out there for?'

Rosie drains an entire glass of soda before responding.

'Less than 30 minutes,' she mumbles, pulling a plastic chair next to the counter and slumping down into it.

'Well, sweat's always a good sign of progress,' he says, gesturing to her face, caked with perspiration.

'Yeah,' Rosie says off-handedly, filling her second glass of soda.

'It's been a while; don't push yourself too–'

'Dad!'

'Oh, I–'

'No, look!'

Rosie's dad whips around to face a frothing pot, hot foam bubbling through the lid and onto the stove. 'Oh dear,' he mutters, quickly reducing the heat.

'You're making pasta?' Rosie asks.

'Trying to,' her dad replies, removing the lid. Blinded by steam, he carefully reaches in with a wooden spoon to retrieve a few macaroni pieces and drops them in his hand. With a hiss of pain, he quickly eats them.

'Still not done, seriously?' He exclaims while chewing, half-amused, half-exasperated. 'Rosie-Dosie-,' Rosie winces slightly, '-would you mind getting the plates out?'

'O.K.'

As Rosie opens the top cabinet, she notices a pan with several charred husks of meat on the counter below.

'Oh, that's the chicken for the pasta,' her dad explains. 'Well, it was chicken. The pan made it charcoal.'

Friday, July 28th - 7:13 AM

Rosie wakes up suddenly. Her eyes easily adjust to the morning light seeping in through her curtains. Despite her aching legs, she feels rather...rested.

That's not right.

Her duvet and bed sheets go *swish,* as she springs out of bed and grabs her phone from her desk.

'How long did I-oh.'

'Seven-fourteen.' Her clock reads. *'Thank God,'* Rosie thinks, relieved.

Turning back towards her bed, she stops in her tracks.

'Y' know, now that I'm already up, I guess...'

Wednesday, August 2nd - 10:05 AM

Dribble, dribble, dribble, step, step, bounce.

Dribble, dribble, dribble, step, step, bounce.

Rosie clicks her tongue in frustration as the basketball drops from the backboard to the pavement, missing the hoop completely.

She grabs the basketball and goes through the lay-up steps in sequence.

Dribble, dribble, dribble.

The basketball bounces off the pavement.

Step, step.

She hops towards the basket, releasing the ball lightly from her right hand.

Swish!

Picking up the basketball from underneath the hoop before going for another lay-up Rosie can't help but smile. Yeah, she's only gotten it once, but it's progress.

Dribble, dribble, dribble, step, step, swish!

Dribble, dribble, dribble, step, step, swish!

Three times. Five times. Nine times. The same movements, the same mechanics, the same results. An odd miss here and there but-

'I'm getting somewhere,' Rosie thinks.

Friday, August 11th - 2:35 PM

'Ugh!'

Despite all her attempts, no matter how she adjusts her shots, Rosie can't seem to make a basket. Retrieving a failed free-throw from underneath the car, she heads back for one more attempt.

'Why is this so much harder?' she complains, reflecting on the easy baskets she made on the same driveway two years prior. When she used to play with...

Rosie shakes herself out of her brooding.

Feet spread out. Right arm tucked. Eyes fixed on the inside of the hoop.

Ready, aim, shoot.

Follow through.

And...

'Wow!'

Rosie turns around. 'Oh, hi Dad.'

'You're really getting good at this!' Her dad says encouragingly. 'Not that you weren't good before but-'

'It was just one basket,' Rosie notes, flustered.

'Hey, one basket can win a game.'

'Yeah.'

Silence fills the driveway for a few moments.

'Uh —how about we play a game?' Rosie's dad asks.

'Maybe tomorrow,' Rosie offers, wiping a few drops of sweat from her forehead.

'Don't want to embarrass your old man, huh?' Her dad jokes.

'It's not you I don't want to embarrass, Dad.'

Saturday, August 19th - 5:50 PM

With calm determination; Rosie dribbles towards the basket.

'You're not getting past the Iron Curtain!' Her dad growls with a mock gruff voice, his legs and arms spread wide.

Laughing, Rosie simultaneously passes the basketball between her dad's legs and leaps forward. Her father turns around, but it's too late. Grabbing the ball with her left hand; she goes for a layup. Easy bucket.

'Guess the Iron Curtain is a bit rusty,' Rosie comments, smirking.

The sun slowly descends as father and daughter keep on playing. For a moment, the neighborhood is once again filled with sounds of laughter and the bounce of the basketball against the concrete of the driveway.

'Whew,' Rosie's dad breathes as she makes another basket. He checks his watch. 'Seven o' clock already!' He exclaims.

'Aw, don't give up yet Dad,' Rosie says, lightly brushing off the sweat from her face.

'I'd better get started on dinner. Want to come in?'

'Nah, I'll hang out here for a little while.'

Her dad ruffles her hair. 'Rosie-Dosie, the basketball robot. You'll be the MVP of your school team for sure.'

'Assuming I get in,' Rosie thinks.

Tuesday, September 26th - 6:30 AM

Rosie stumbles into the kitchen. Despite her recently completed workout, her body is still loading. The salty smell of sizzling sausages energizes her slightly.

'Morning Rosie-Dosie!' her dad says, turning to give her a smile before facing the pan.

'Looks gre-eat Dad,' Rosie yawns.

'Thought I'd make you a special breakfast,' her dad explains as she pours a glass of water. 'Just like your mother-'

Rosie feels a chill unrelated to the ice-cold water she just drank. Her mind freezes. Her emotions crash.

Rosie's dad's face falls slowly. 'Oh Rosie, I didn't...'

'It's fine Dad,' Rosie mumbles, feeling a bit more tired than before.

A solemn silence follows.

'W-when do you need to be at school?' Rosie's dad asks.

Tuesday, September 26th - 3:45 PM

Classes concluded; the real struggle begins.

Rosie nervously scans the basketball court, the *squees'* of sneakers on wooden floors and the chatter of teenage girls filling the hall. Clutching her bag tightly, she makes her way toward the other girls. Some are taller than her, some are shorter, but almost all of them seem more confident.

'I wish Dad was here,' Rosie mutters.

'I wish Mom was here too,' she thinks.

Her breathing becomes more rapid. *'Oh I can't do this.'*

In a panic, she turns around to head back to the safety of the changing room. But then, as if someone placed a recording in her mind-

'Game time Rosie,' she remembers.

She pauses.

Despite her anxiety, Rosie turns back towards the challenge.

Warm-ups, layups, free-throws, pick-and-rolls, Rosie is on a roll.

'This is easy!' she thinks, as she sidesteps another girl and heads towards the basket. *'This is great!'*

With the ball firmly in her hands, she attempts her first

shot of the practice game.

Swish.

She misses. The ball lightly brushes against the net.

Embarrassed, Rosie turns towards the coach, who scribbles a note down on her clipboard and continues to observe.

When tryouts end, Rosie's heart rate continues to rise. Everything was going well until that first shot. Then she just *had* to air ball three shots in a row.

Rosie fidgets with her bag strap as Coach Amanda paces up and down the line of girls.

All those early mornings and late evenings. Hours of practice. Wasted.

'No game is a wasted one,' she remembers Mom telling her after a bad game at home. *'You'll always gain something.'*

Rosie closes her eyes and takes a deep breath.

'Well girls,' Coach Amanda begins. 'Let's get right down to business...'

Thursday, October 19th - 7:30 PM

'First game tomorrow!' Rosie's dad exclaims with pride. 'Are you excited?'

Rosie half-smirks as she cuts into her steak. 'I'm only playing because Min sprained her ankle,' she reminds him.

'That's still great!' Her Dad points out. 'You playing; that is, not Min getting injured.'

'I'll probably not be that good.'

'You don't know that.'

'It might be my only game Dad.'

'Well, even if it is your only game in a while, why not try and make it the best game that you can?'

Rosie's retort dies in her throat as she gulps down her potatoes. She looks opposite her, facing an empty space.

Where a third chair used to be.

'Rosie, look-'.

'Dad...'

He tenderly takes her hand.

Rosie feels her heart constricting.

But she can't ignore it anymore.

'It's been so hard!' She admits, her voice cracking. 'All of it! Training. Without Mom. She always used to-I mean; you play with me too but—'

Her dad's grip tightens, but in a secure sort of way.

'I-I just miss her,' she stammers, starting to cry.

Rosie's dad moves his chair right next to her. Putting his arm around her, they look at the empty space. Together.

'I miss her too,' Rosie's dad says, blinking rapidly.

He looks at her with grief, but loving determination.

'But she'd want us to be happy. She'd want *you* to be happy.

And you're happy when you play, yeah?'

Sniffling slightly, Rosie nods.

'So was she. So am I.'

Friday, October 20th - 4:30 PM

'DE-FENCE!'

'DE-FENCE!'

The crowd chants in sync as the final seconds of the game ebb away. There's less than half a minute left.

The score: 30-29. Rosie's team are trailing behind.

Sasha passes to Naomi; Naomi tries to make a shot. Blocked.

Ayen grabs the ball but is quickly swarmed by defenders.

Ten seconds left.

Ayen scans the court. Desperately, she flings the ball to…

Seven seconds left.

Rosie gets the pass.

Six seconds left.

'Hey, one basket can win a game,' she remembers.

She doesn't look at the stands, but she knows he's watching her.

She's watching her, too.

Five seconds left.

Roberto Oduor

The defenders move towards her, but it's too late. Muscle memory sets in. Rosie's already airborne.

The basketball leaves her hands and arcs towards the hoop.

Three…two…

Swish.

The Train to Retirement

By Yulia Zasorenko

Michael had been looking forward to this day for months. After graduating from university with a degree in Accounting, he finally secured his first employment opportunity at a prestigious accounting firm in London. Initially walking into the underground station, his excitement and nerves made his heart race.

Seeing an appropriate train, he jogged aboard and sat by a window. He was surrounded by a sea of faces in the crowded carriage, each absorbed in their thoughts and ideas. The smell of perfume and sweat filled the air, and his ears were drilled with chatter and brakes screeching.

Michael felt confined as the doors closed, and the train started to whistle as it moved again. He had never enjoyed crowds, so the thought of being ensnared in a metal tube with dozens of strangers made him uneasy.

Yulia Zasorenko

Michael attempted to distract himself as the train accelerated by gazing out the window. The city was a blur of grey buildings and bustling streets, with occasional glimpses of green parks and open spaces. He looked at the flurry of people who were lost in their worlds and had their faces hidden by masks and limbs.

Michael started to think about his new job. For so long, he had studied and prepared for this, and now it was finally upon him. He felt excitement and anxiety as he considered the challenges ahead. Would he be able to fulfil the requirements of the job? Would he get along with the people he works with? His thoughts engulfed him as the train sped through the gloom.

A new group of people got on when the train stopped at a station. Michael started to feel more and more anxious as the train got busier. As he felt the weight of the other passengers pressing into him, he found himself pushed against the damp and cold window.

As he heard the train vibrating beneath him and the rhythmic sound of the wheels on the tracks, his breathing began to slow down. As soon as the train started moving again, Michael tried to relax. He exhaled deeply, closed his eyes, and focused on his chest's movement.

The train became emptier as the journey continued, and Michael felt relieved. Moving his arms and legs gave him a sense of freedom he hadn't had since getting on the train.

Nerves started taking over once more as Michael approached his destination. He smoothed his hair and straightened his tie to project confidence. He checked his watch to make sure he was on time.

The Train to Retirement

Michael emerged onto the platform when the train finally arrived at the station. As the cold air hit him like a blow to the face, he took a deep breath and felt excited about his upcoming adventure.

While making his way toward his new workplace, Michael was filled with pride and a sense of accomplishment. He had made it to his first job, and he was ready to deal with any challenges that might come his way. He had reminded himself of his capabilities, contrary to the ongoing and never-ending intrusive thoughts.

He experienced a blur of new faces, further information, and new responsibilities on his first day at his new job. As he rode the subway home, he couldn't help but recall the day's events.

He lost himself in thought as he stared out the window in the less crowded carriage this time. Even though he is the centre of his world, others do not seem to notice him on this occasion. He had always wanted to be an accountant. After getting his first job, he couldn't help but wonder if it was really what he wanted to do.

Taking in the world around him, Michael's thoughts began to wander. Did he meet the requirements for this position? Although working for such a prestigious company put alot of pressure on him, he had always been good with numbers. He already had the impression that he was submerged in a sea of paperwork despite only being there for one day.

Michael was knocked out of his mind by the screeching of the breaks when the train stopped at the next station. He noticed that people were getting on and off the train quickly, and as they did so, their faces became blurry. He thought he was a tiny cog in a much larger and more intricate machine. Was this something he wanted for the rest of his life?

The train left the station and Michael began to experience a growing sense of unease. He considered his college buddies, who were pursuing their passions and goals. Some took trips worldwide, started businesses, or even returned to school to learn more. As he sat on a train returning to his cramped apartment, he dreaded repeating everything the following day.

Michael observed as passengers boarded the train at a different station. He felt he was in a different world, one with deadlines and spreadsheets, and he wasn't sure if that was the kind of world he wanted to be in. He thought about how his parents had always helped him reach his goals. Was this his dream?

He knew that he needed to decide as soon as the train started moving again. Did he prefer to continue on this path or pursue a different one? Changing courses and pursuing a diverse career or interest could be a viable option. For him, there was a glimmer of hope and a sense of fear and uncertainty.

Once the train approached his stop, Michael got off and returned to his apartment. He had the impression that he was about to make a big decision that would improve his life. He knew he had to work hard to figure out the future, even though he wasn't sure what it would bring.

Michael's thoughts were still focused on his first day at work as he fell into a restless slumber that night. He saw a never-ending pile of paperwork and looming deadlines in his dream. He saw his co-workers examine him critically as if they could sense his fears. Michael was submerged in a sea of numbers

The Train to Retirement

and formulas, struggling to keep his head above water. He tried to escape, but the more he fought, the further he was crushed. He had the impression that he was being choked out and caught up in a world in which he had no place.

When Michael awoke, he was drenched in sweat and had a racing heart. He got out of bed and stood up, overwhelmed and disoriented. He realised that he had been clenching his teeth all night and felt tension in his jaw. Michael's doubts and ambiguities were returning. He imagined being viewed as a failure, losing his job, and disappointing his friends and family.

Although he knew he could not ignore his problems forever, he briefly considered calling in sick. He took a deep breath and got out of bed, determined to face the day ahead. He washed, changed, and made himself a cup of coffee, hoping that the caffeine would help him relax.

As Michael made his way to the subway station, he started feeling a build-up of fear. The nightmare lingered over him like a gloomy cloud despite his efforts to forget about it. He wondered if he was making a mistake because he had chosen the wrong path. He asked himself if he had the intelligence or determination to succeed in this position.

As he boarded the train, he found himself looking at his fellow commuters' faces to see if they were experiencing the same emotions as he was. He believed he was the only one trying to figure out where he belonged.

Michael took a deep breath when the train pulled up to his stop. He tried eliminating the unease, but it stayed with him like a second skin. He didn't know what the day would bring when he went to the office.

As he got off the train and onto the platform, Michael's thoughts were consumed by memories of a traumatic incident on the tube several years earlier.

During the crowded rush hour, Michael could barely squeeze onto the train. As he was pressed against the door, his face was just inches away from the glass. The train entered a tunnel with a sudden jolt, and the lights went out.

Michael had felt a wave of panic wash over him as the train stopped. He tried to get through the crowd, but he was unable to move. The sound of breathing and the smell of sweat permeated the air, giving Michael the impression that he was being suffocated.

As time went on, Michael felt his anxiety grow. He believed he would be sick. His chest was pounding as he tried to focus on breathing. The darkness was oppressive, and he could feel himself merging with the metal, becoming invisible to other passengers. Eventually, some of the passengers got off the train and it started moving after what seemed like forever. Michael stumbled and shook his legs. Never before had he felt so helpless and vulnerable.

That experience caused Michael to develop a fear of the tube. The mere thought of being trapped in a dim, crowded space sent his anxiety skyrocketing. He walked or took the bus, avoiding the subway at all costs.

However, he was aware that when he started his new job as an accountant, he would have to deal with his anxiety. Walking or taking the bus would take too long to get to his office, which was in the city's heart. As a result, he gradually forced himself to use the tube daily.

The Train to Retirement

Michael was aware of the challenges ahead when he walked into the office after getting off the train. He also knew that he had the strength to face them one step at a time.

Michael had made it, to an extent. He realised that the rat race had begun, which he voluntarily entered. Now, his happiness was tied to the size of his apartment and the acceleration time of his car. Material possessions will now dictate his satisfaction with life.

The beginning was torture. Michael would spend the entire journey grabbing the handrails as his heart raced. When he could get off the train, his legs would be numb with relief.

But over time, he started to see a change. As he continued to ride the tube, his anxiety diminished. He became more at ease in the small space; breathing became an easier task and the people around him didn't seem to be as close and overbearing.

As he became more accustomed to the tube, he also began to pay attention to the people around him. He began to converse with strangers on the train and felt a sense of community. He felt less isolated as a result, although it wasn't much.

Michael now felt proud when he entered the office. He was victorious after overcoming his fear. He had proved to himself that he was more talented than he realised.

Violent Tendencies

By Jasmine Collins

She woke up. The cube was white.

A pair of fluorescent bars hung above her bed - their hum had become a friendly accompaniment to her morning routine. The sanitised light bounced off the Perspex walls and illuminated the room; a rather sparse space, but she wasn't fussed by it. Of course, it had taken a little getting used to living here when compared with things before, but with a constant workflow and a strict routine she soon didn't think twice about where she was.

She sat up and rubbed her eyes, ready to commence her morning routine. This was something she'd started the second year she'd lived in the Cube: to take note of everything in the room and give thanks to CosmoCorp for providing such an adequate work-live arrangement. At the far side of her room, there was a small desk with a computer currently open on a set of spreadsheets for the company's upcoming quarterly review. A wheely chair was tucked neatly underneath. It was here that she spent sixteen hours a day, every day, for the rest of her life if she was lucky.

Above the desk, there was a poster with a group of ethnically diverse individuals all in a bout of shared laughter - the words 'WORK HARD. BE GREAT.' above their heads. She imagined what it would be like to have friends of her own. They could go on team-building retreats. They could build a campfire and roast marshmallows. They could tell each other their deepest, darkest secrets in a tent under the stars. Though it occurred to her that she didn't really know what she'd say? That she'd messed up last year's expense review, blamed it on Jerry and he'd been swiftly terminated? Yeah, she'd go with that one.

To the left of her desk was a water cooler and a coffee machine, with a neat stack of five paper cups between them. She never ran out of paper cups, even on her 'Crazy Thursdays', where she allowed herself three cups of coffee instead of two. If she had the time to consider the implications of this; unknown individuals entering her cube while she slept for the sole purpose of replacing the cups- she might have begun to question her entire situation. However today, as was the case every day, her mind wasn't focused on this. Instead, it was on her morning sustenance.

Right on cue, a small buzz filled the room, signalling the beginning of a plastic capsule's daily journey down the delivery chute. She watched as it snaked its way through the translucent piping on the wall before arriving on her desk. She twisted it open. Inside she found a NutraFun™ bar and a HappyTime™ pill.[1] She grabbed a cup, filled it up with water

---

1   Use HappyTime Inc. products at your own discretion. HappyTime Inc. is not responsible for any dissociation, delusions or loss of sanity that may occur when our products are used.

and took her breakfast. It was banana flavoured; she preferred strawberry. She began her work. She was fine.

She woke up. The cube was white.

As she opened her eyes, she shot a glance towards her computer clock. Today was the 31st. A large toothy grin suddenly crossed her face. Today was the day they announced the next 'employee of the month' for her section of the company. She'd won it four times since she'd entered the Cube, which was second only to Simon in accounting. She hated Simon in accounting. His *five* wins were the talk of the office, being proudly displayed in his company Slack banner. These gave him the opportunity to be featured in the company's internal training videos. Their sole purpose was to reaffirm the ethos and direction of the company, whilst showing workers how to be a, 'valued member of the CosmoCorp family'. They would always end with a shot of an enthusiastic Simon, a plastic smile on his face. The voiceover praised his selflessness and dedication to the company - asking each employee to 'succeed like Simon'. She loathed him. She had recently started to respond to him with only a simple 'regards' at the end of emails, confident he would pick up on the savagery of the gesture. Though perhaps it wasn't hatred she felt, so much as a deep jealousy of Simon. He was consistently recognised for his work, while it would seem all her efforts were just fleeting attempts to gain similar validation from the second largest corporation in the United States.

Though, she reminded herself, if she got today's 'Employee of the Month' award none of this would matter - she would have the (joint) highest number of accolades in the office and her life would have meaning.

Considering all of this, she walked over to the coffee machine for her morning brew. Lost in thought, she filled the cup too high and poured scalding hot liquid onto her hand. She yelped and dropped the cup, which bounced gently on the floor. It was strange - she hadn't felt pain like this in a long time. She took a moment and tried to recall the last time she had felt a similar pain and landed on a memory of her previous job where she had accidentally fried her hand on a burger grill.

Well, she said it was accidental but the act was, in fact, quite deliberate. A building desire to get off work early had led her to the impulsive act. She'd been skipping more and more, coming up with excuse after excuse – though once you lose five grandparents within the span of a month, people start to get a little suspicious. She thought frying her hand would be a good way to garner pity from her boss and give her a couple of weeks off if it was bad enough. She did indeed get to go home early, though she was fired a week later.

It had been dumb luck that she stumbled into her new life in the Cube. She'd seen an advert on TikTok about an all-expenses-paid, live-in position at CosmoCorp. All it took was an NDA and a couple of simple injections, easy stuff to get out of her tiny, damp flat. She'd gone to the induction day, blacked out, and woke up in her new home with a strong drive to work and a deep love of spreadsheets. She'd started on her journey up the CosmoCorporate ladder and couldn't wait to make a difference. However, now looking back on her past life, she struggled to recognise the person she once was. In fact, most of her memories from before her life in the Cube were fuzzy - almost like she saw them through a pane of frosted glass. The more she tried to recall them the more disjointed they became, and she was left struggling to separate what was real and what was fake.

She also had difficulty establishing an emotional connection to her past self, often taking an overly critical stance against her actions. Before the Cube, she'd been lazy and selfish and had done nothing with her life. She'd wasted all the opportunities she'd been given. She was a waste of potential. But personal growth had to count for something? Right? Her new life had worth, and she'd be damned if she had to go back to that place and lose it all. Since she entered the Cube she had no more emotional outbursts, though she also couldn't remember the last time she was truly happy. It was at this moment that she realised she'd been standing by the coffee machine, her head full of unproductive thoughts and her hand pulsating with pain, for the past five minutes. This wouldn't do. She poured herself a cup of water, submerged her hand until it stopped throbbing, and started her work. She was fine.

An hour later she stopped typing. Her food capsule hadn't arrived and there was a low gurgling in her stomach. Hunger was another feeling she hadn't experienced in several years. The all-in-one NutraFun™ bars she received twice daily were designed by a team of leading nutritionists to be the perfect accompaniment to the workday. The bar is small enough to fit in all brands of sustenance capsule but they are always big on flavour. There's no more need to worry about messy meals, when you can get your hands on a NutraFun™ Bar! And it now occurred to her that, yes, they were indeed all she had eaten for the past seven years of her life. Choice was rather difficult after all, and if the guiding hand of her corporate superiors could help her make one less decision every day, that must be a positive change to her life.

Another hour passed, and then another. Still no sign of her capsule. It occurred to her that she didn't actually know how else she would be able to acquire sustenance if it didn't roll down her wall and arrive on her desk. This was all she had ever known during her time here and she didn't want it to change. Change was scary. Perhaps she could eat one of her cups? They were marked as biodegradable, after all. She hoped things wouldn't get to that point. She pondered this throughout the day until she'd completed all the work assigned to her. Still no capsule. Had she been forgotten? Was she not working hard enough to earn the sustenance she needed? And to top it all off, there was no mention of this month's 'Employee of the Month'. These thoughts danced around her head as she drifted into an uneasy unconsciousness.

She woke up. The cube was red.

This perplexed her. She'd never seen it like this, not once in all the years she had lived in the cube. She walked over to her computer to begin her day, but it didn't turn on. She frowned, it had never had any faults and was always in perfect working order. She weighed her options. She could sit there and wait for it to turn on, (though she had no idea how long that could take), or she could leave the cube via the sliding doorway in the wall. In her seven years at CosmoCorp she'd never left the confines of the cube before, though of course, she'd never needed to. Everything she had ever needed to survive was delivered remotely to her. She was able to continue living indefinitely in the home she had created for herself - until now it would appear.

Her stomach rumbled again, accompanied by dull aching and general fatigue. This wouldn't do. She couldn't possibly complete her daily tasks like that, especially not with a broken computer. As she couldn't reach any higher-ups electronically, the only reasonable course of action was to find a higher authority in person. She approached the doorway and stepped through. Immediately she was met by a long corridor stretching to her left and right. On the wall, someone had scrawled:

'THEY ARE DEAD. WE ARE THE ONLY ONES LEFT.'

She didn't know who this mystery graffiti artist was referring to, but she was not best pleased they had defaced company property. Something screamed in the distance, followed by a series of gunshots which made her jump. This was the first time she'd heard a voice other than her own in all the time she'd spent in the facility. She would have felt comfort in the presence of fellow human beings, though this feeling was largely overshadowed by a sense of immediate danger. Why would someone bring a gun here? Shaking at the thought of what would happen if she did nothing, she tentatively made her way in the direction of the noise.

As she progressed down the corridor, she tried to access every door she could. Many opened to reveal cubes much like her own, all seemingly vacated and left in various states of disarray. The first she found seemed to be nearly identical to her own cube, right down to the stack of five paper cups by the coffee machine. There was a thick layer of dust coating the space and a heavy musk in the air.

The second cube she found was in a much worse state than the first. A foul-smelling stream of black liquid trickled out of a crack in the ceiling and coated the floor. The smell made her rather nauseous; she decided to leave quickly. Everything inside the third cube had been broken. The thin, wooden desk had been split in two, and everything that had been on top of it – the computer, peripherals, paperwork – were strewn across the floor. The water cooler and surrounding Perspex walls all had large dents in them as if they had been struck with a sizable blunt object. However, there was still no sign of human life.

Other doors down the corridor led to simple closets, filled with mops, bleach and other assorted cleaning supplies. She passed a couple of empty conference rooms too. These were relic of an earlier time, when people would meet in person and talk about company comings-and-goings, rather than using the more time-efficient email and Slack systems. The mentality was that there was no time wasted travelling to and from such places, which could better be spent actually working. CosmoCorp generated $1.2 trillion annually, so a six-minute walk to and from a conference would generate unnecessary losses in the millions.

The shouts had become distant. She kept walking until she saw a door unlike any other. It had a simple plaque on it which read, 'Managing Director'. It had been clearly opened with force, with damage to the wall around it, and it remained open.

She stepped through the threshold into the dimly lit room. A balding man in an expensive suit lay face-down on a large mahogany table. His face was angled away from the door, and a dim blue glow from a nearby computer gave a hint to the outline of his figure. There was a cascade of spreadsheets and other paperwork trailing off the desk and covering the carpeted floor.

She took a deep breath and tentatively approached the man, noticing his chest rising and falling, accompanied by a low rasping sound. As she rounded the corner of the desk, he slowly pulled himself upright – the effort to do so generating a guttural moan from deep within him. As his wide, bloodshot eyes met hers, his breathing intensified and he began to whimper.

She looked him up and down, now with a better view of his upright figure. His wrists and ankles had been bound to the chair with duct tape. The insides of his arms faced upwards and had long lacerations down their length. The splayed fabric and flesh were coated in a deep crimson. Beneath him was a pool of congealing blood. His thighs had dozens of stab wounds through his tattered grey suit. A letter opener remained upright in his left thigh. Two bullet holes penetrated his expensive suit: one in his left shoulder and the other in his chest which seemed to have punctured a lung if his rasping breaths were any indication.

All she could do was stare, dumbfounded, unable to break eye contact with the man. After a moment, he gingerly opened his blood-soaked mouth and began to repeatedly moan, 'peas, peas helf'.

She assumed he meant 'please' rather than expressing a fondness for spherical, green vegetables, but what could she actually do to help this gentleman. He struggled against his restraints with what little strength he had left and gestured with his head towards the desk. On it sat another letter opener next to a large novelty mug filled with coffee that read, 'WORLD'S BEST BOSS'. She reached for the blade, but something else had also caught her eye. It was his desk plate.

Alan A. Pierce

Managing Director

Violent Tendencies

She stopped; eyes fixated on the small piece of engraved gold in front of her. *Alan A. Pierce. Managing Director. Managing. Director.* She wasn't entirely sure what a managing director did, but it sounded like a role with a lot of responsibilities. Managing – like manager? She'd make a great manager. She always had ideas about how to improve the efficiency of her team and people said she had great people skills too. And director? Like to direct? She could take the company in a whole new direction. Well, Alan over here couldn't possibly do that in his current state now, could he? He's strapped to a chair, losing so much blood. To be honest, that isn't very leader-like at all. A leader should be strong and capable and be able to take on any challenge that comes their way. This showing from him had been rather pathetic, to be honest. His behaviour had reflected poorly on CosmoCorp, and therefore she'd have to make sure it wouldn't happen again.

She pulled out the letter opener and turned towards him. He'd slouched over and his breathing had become even more strained. He didn't even have the strength to raise his head. She plunged the length of the blade into his neck. He squirmed, there was a spurt of blood, then he went still. She pulled it out and cut his bindings. He fell out of the chair in a battered pile.

As she took in the scene, she spied a familiar object on the ground which had rolled a little way away from the desk. She reached down and picked it up. It was a sustenance capsule. She quickly opened it and ate its contents, swishing down the HappyTime™ pill with the leftover coffee in the mug.[2] It was a more flavourful blend than she was used to, with a rich complexity she hadn't tasted in a long time. Beneath the gore that covered the desk, she spotted a landline telephone with

---

2   HappyTime Inc. has proven in a court of law that our products do not contribute to violent tendencies.

a few speed-dial options. She found the 'CLEANING' button and pressed it and was put through to Nicola in cleaning, who would be up right away. She took her seat in the now vacated chair. It had excellent lumbar support. She connected the keyboard and found the mouse. She began her work.

She was fine.

The Rules are Different at Sea

By Blakeney Clark

Captain Arras holds the compass in an outstretched gloved hand. The needle ticks and quivers in its box, jumping from north, northeast to north, northwest; then back to the tiny illustration of a sea monster, marking north. The beast's features are distorted by a drop of rain that has fallen and clung there.

The *Tranquillitas,* great vessel that she is, barely shivers as the next wave parts around the bow. Through the fog the water is purplish black, and the sea, strangely subdued as it laps around the dark floating islands on its surface.

There is money in that water, the captain thinks. The kind of money of the likes none of the crew have seen in their lives before. Rich folk in the city would pay highly for the elixir that lit their petroleum lamps; the light to see by, read by, tell stories by. And money was earned through shares not wages.

Hidden by the mist, a rare smile hovers at his lips. There is a strange fervour building in the air ever since the first sighting, even as the work is hard and the air is stinging and acrid with smoke - it was exciting.

Snapping the compass shut, the captain's attention is caught by the quiet *scree-scree* of metal on wood, coming from behind a pile of netting. Scrubber, the youngest of the crewmen, is hunched atop an old float, tongue between his teeth in concentration, whittling a piece of bone out of sight of Arras's post. Naturally so. Idleness was one of the captain's three I's of punishable offence - as well as insolence and insubordination (which handily covered anything which irritated the captain in the moment).

Is it supposed to be a boot? The captain wonders. He sidles closer. A fish? Perhaps a badly moulded porpoise with its head caved in?

Turning around to see him there, Scrubber flinches. There isn't a lot of free time to be had upon the *Tranquillitas*. With the decks still washed in red and harpoons lying in need of cleaning before they rust, he has no excuse to be sitting around doing nothing and by the expression on his face he knows it.

For half a second the captain regrets having caught him.

But the quietude of the moment is lost and Arras's expression hardens in familiar reprimand. The captain once again feels the distance fall between them.

'Sorry sir!' Scrubber blurts, jamming the bone and knife into his belt. Arras has just enough time to see what it is. A knobbly heart, a luckenbooth; a love token popular in Scotland. He'd forgotten that. That Scrubber has a home somewhere. A lover, a name. The rules were different at sea and the unspoken policy told in looks and silent meals was that you left your old self behind. The reminder of Scrubber's life back at home is an unpleasant one and the captain snaps back to himself.

'Get back to work,' he shouts, 'You know every moment is precious during reaping's. You're lucky I don't give you a flogging!'

Red faced and chastened, the boy stumbles away. But there is a glint in his eyes that the captain doesn't like, something greedy and resentful. And his gaze lingers on the captain's gold buttons and damask coat as he joins the rest of the crew on deck.

There is a muttering from the stern as the men close ranks, glancing up from their tasks. Each move with restlessness. Uninterested in the trivialities of cleaning and recuperating supplies when their blood still sings for the thrill of the hunt. In their minds they are re-living the days that came before, still riding the high that floods a man with a sense of unbridled power. One or two shoot resentful looks in the captain's direction. Their appetite for action is insatiable and they do not hide their annoyance at this return to serfhood. These hours of nothingness breed nothing but trouble.

It is the golden rule of captaincy to monitor that simmering resentment in the air, and Captain Arras prided himself on striking the balance between inspiring fear, respect, and taking the biggest share of the pie so to speak. There was more slippage between ranks while at sea and you heard stories on the wind of captains' overthrown by a covetous crew – whether to the waves, or worse, to the indignity of cabin-boy drudgery.

As a result his style was showy, calculated, impressive but

he worried that his growing paunch made him the butt of jokes behind the men's backs. The fat that had accumulated from the best cuts of salt meat and the largest ration of saltine was a visible reminder of their subordinance to him. For the most part he trusted his men, but during the reaping's they got a taste for power and new ideas of riches came into their heads. As the seas grew blacker with blood and with oil, the lines between man and monster blurred.

'Stellar Sea Cow!' The voice, hoarse with sudden excitement, comes from the crow's nest. It's Dugon, the ship's spotter and he leans precariously down, suddenly charged with energy. There is a clatter as the crew drop their tools and their ears perk up at the sighting of their next quarry.

'It's right ahead, dead north, do you see?' Captain Arras rushes back to the ship's bow along with the rest of the crew and plugs a brass telescope to his eye.

'There!'

'No, to the left!'

'I see it!'

'I don't!'

The men speculate on the creature's weight, size, and value before it can surface again. Caught up in the fervour, the captain has to take a moment to focus on the task at hand. He realises his telescope is the wrong way round and, hoping no one has noticed, he corrects it and scans the sea.

The waters are full of bodies. Looming humpback islands (bristling with harpoons like flagpoles), bloated manatees plundered beyond recognition, and between them, obscured

The Rules are Different at Sea

by the mist, smaller lumps of mangled red and grey which had once been fur seals. The journey had been profitable of late.

His attention is caught by a sudden spray of water and the flick of a thick, muscular tail. Fumbling in excitement; he swings the telescope round, twists it to bring the blurred outline into focus, and catches his breath.

She is magnificent. Dark silver and big as a schooner. Her whole body seemingly an extension of the tail, moving together in slow strokes. The head is strangely small and spade-like compared to her massive girth, promising the kind of subcutaneous fat that would fill the coffers of every man aboard.

A strange stillness overtakes the boat. Each man knew what sort of discovery a Stellar Sea Cow was. Not only were they valuable but they were also rare. No one had seen one for years and the bragging rights would earn them fame on top of fortune back in England. What if this was the last Stellar Sea Cow? What if it were this very ship, the humble *Tranquillitas*, which brought the prize home? All thirty feet of her carefully packaged in geometrical squares with the tail and head pinned to the gunwale.

Captain Arras's eyes gleam. With a sudden burst of animalistic energy the men are scrambling about the deck, a machine well-oiled in the art of violence. Captain Arras swings himself into the rigging, hoarsely giving orders, a manic gleam in his eye. Then, when he can resist the temptation no more, he slips in with the rest of them. His fingers close around a barbed harpoon and he snatches the cruellest looking pike from the cask maker, eager to join the hunt.

The time for words is left somewhere behind and the men communicate in hoarse cries.

'The sea cow is in sight!'

Closer, closer, and then at the last minute, as if becoming aware of the men's attention, the great beast turns to them and lets out a low groan of confused greeting.

Then – *thwack!* The first harpoon is fired, crashing into the water besides her.

Startled, she dives – but too late! *Thwopp!* The next harpoon finds its mark. The long rope it trails behind is fixed to the ship and as she struggles the *Tranquillitas* lurches as if in sympathy.

Hollering and hooting sounds across the deck as the men let loose their arsenal. The captain gives himself up to the thrill of it, forgetting his rank, forgetting even his name, he pushes amidst the mob crowded on the starboard side, throwing his own lance (which falls hopelessly into the sea), and pike (which finds its mark). He whoops triumphantly, chest welling with pride to have made his mark in the melee.

Soon the animal resembles a hedgehog, its quills a mismatch of thick harpoons, black barbs, and even the cook's kitchen knives, thrown in a paroxysm of violence. It bellows and moans in chorus with the men's whoops.

The captain watches in anticipation as a rowing boat is dispatched to bring the monster in, and once she is winched aboard and lain out (taking up the whole length of the deck), the men set upon her.

The blubber, the fat, the thick, white layers of her peeling away like a present. The gold in that flesh, the precision and care within the frenzy with which the carnage is performed. Perhaps they are predatory animals? But this crew are also profiteers, and it shows in the quasi-worship of the blubber as it is cut from bone.

All the same, the men are boys at heart, and boys must be allowed their fun. So the death is not a short one and the white squares are cut from the animal as she lies alive and obscurely still, observing the action with sad, frightened eyes.

The captain didn't mean to meet those eyes. It was more difficult to enjoy the work so much that way, yet somehow, he couldn't help but feel drawn to them. Up close the face was still more strange. Wrinkled and flat like a bull dog's, with dark coal lumps for eyes peering up at him beneath folds of pockmarked skin. He felt the same guilt he would feel looking into the face of God.

The thought is new and unsettling and the captain feels an uncomfortable prickling of self-awareness, taking him out of the enjoyment of the moment. 'It is this fog,' he tells himself, 'Everyone knows sea mist this thick has a hallucinatory effect.'

He wipes his blade on his trousers and with difficulty, looks away.

'You're very valuable,' he says and isn't entirely sure why he says it. He is uncomfortably aware that his gloves, the deck, the rope, and his coat are all sticky and slippery with blood.

The crew are up to their arms in it, the white of the blubber startling against the varying shades of crimson that stain their knives. Nothing distinguishing them from carrion birds, the captain thinks.

***

Across the deck from Captain Arras, the boy that was once called Scrubber looks up from where he is crouched by the body. He is up to his arms in blubber and gore and sways with the intoxication of a primal power. From the corner of his red-tinged vision, he thinks he sees the captain is lurching giddily.

He blinks hazily. It is as if the magnitude that kept the captain on the ground has tripled – quadrupled in strength. As Scrubber watches, his skin seems to droop, dripping down his face like candle wax. His eyes darken, swelling out of his sockets as his jaw works frantically, trying to speak – no... to scream. Before the captain is able to utter a sound his teeth seem to fuse together, and his tongue recedes into his throat.

His body begins to swell. The captain's already thick midriff ripples and oozes, the fat between skin and bone expanding, straining his damask coat. Rows of tiny gold buttons push out until they pop off, *ting, ting, ting,* onto the deck. The noise echoes in Scrubber's head as he stares at them on the planks, struggling to compute the tiny mundane buttons with the incongruity of their arriving there.

As he stares, transfixed, the shadow of the captain grows and grows, out and up. He lifts his eyes to the captain's legs and sees instead, two thick trunks of greyish skin, twisting and melding together into a monstrous, familiar taper.

He yells to get the others' attention. The fog is thick now, the men, dazed with blood. It takes no encouragement for them to see it too.

Their blood frenzy forgotten, they stare in incomprehension – and then fall over themselves to scramble back as the monster towers over them.

Their Captain flops forward onto the deck.

He is ginormous. In length maybe six times as long as he was before. Skin like tree bark, tail a grotesque parody of a mermaid's – grey, thick with muscle; ugly. His body is slug-like, arms like oven mitts. Scrubber notices that the captain's hat is still stuck jauntily upon his misshapen head.

Lying beside the body of the Stellar Sea Cow the similarity between the two is unmistakable. The captain blinks at the Sea Cow and she seems to communicate something back to him through her eyes. Then she is still, and the captain blinks again, this time dumbly,

No more than an animal, Scrubber thinks.

Now there is silence. The wind stops blowing and the drizzle finally abates. The captain stares at the crew and the crew, wordlessly, stares back.

There is a moment then.

A fragile wavering between reason and instinct, between man and beast. A moment when the crew's eyes rest on the thick fat around the captain's middle.

Despite the heady mist, it is suddenly easy to see.

Scrubber is the first to draw his scythe. The rest of the crew gather by.

They are men of profit not sentiment after all. And the blubber of a sea cow is worth its weight in gold.

The compass ticks and the waters around the *Tranquillitas* turn from purple to brightest gold.

After all, anyone who sailed those waters knew, the rules were different at sea.

Home Is Where the Heart Is

By James Albin

Patient: Mr. [Redacted]. Memory #32, 1907

One night, when I was a child, I saw The Old Man Folded Up Beneath The Stairs. Scared at first, by his long fingers, his bulging eyes, his straggly white-grey hair which parted on the top (as though a little Moses were leading his people over the shiny dome of his head) I recoiled. In Poland apparently, they call these men 'Domovoy' – I am not quite sure. I got the overwhelming feeling that what I was seeing was the true man of the house, who had remained undemoted from his strange position despite having watched the passing of countless, clueless families. Either way, he was a little terrifying and exceedingly odd. His eyes were large, deep and dark and seemed neither good nor evil, but malleable.

The Old Man Folded Up Beneath The Stairs...unfolded himself and nonchalantly began hobbling through the corridor, muttering to himself in some unintelligible speech. I paused to consider his grey eyes, like mine, and how he walked in such a determined way towards an unseen goal. What I had done to deserve such a visitation I did not know. Stopping, he looked back at me as though I were a dunce and gestured me follow with one long, hairy finger.

Call me a fool, but I followed him.

At first I thought he was going to the kitchen for leftovers, as, despite his authority, he seemed like the leftover kind, but he continued past the kitchen and down the corridor. Further and further we went, until we were in a part of my corridor that I had never seen before. Turning to the left, he rattled a handle on a little door and opened it.

The basement. *We had a basement?*

Down we went, deeper and deeper. My back ached from bending over while the little old man obliviously trotted forward down the little winding spiral staircase as he had clearly done many times before. I thought to myself that he must only make this passage in the dead of night – when the clocks fear to move. Then he halted, took a single gasp of air, and walked forth out of sight into a great smoky room.

The engine room of the family egregore.

Rattling, huffing, hissing, crashing and moaning before me was a gigantic beating heart. The aorta emitted a trinitarian draconic flame, the pulmonary veins connected to the walls were translucently squeezing black tar · like snakes swallowing industrial material – the left and right ventricles were cages in which canaries manically cried dates, times, and the names of the long-forgotten dead.

I gasped in horror, almost collapsing with fright, turned,

went back up the twisting staircase, up and up, through the peculiar dreamlike door, along the corridor that never was, past the kitchen, past the cranny under the stairs and up into bed. I tried to put it out of my mind, and never went looking for the Domovoy again.

A Comment On this Curious Document

Since Darwin we have been dimly aware of the awful shadows of atavistic shapes moving in our psyche. And since the great Idealists we have been even more aware of that terrifying knowledge which is the absolute interdependence of human persons. It seems to us in this unsure age that our individual selves are but the tip of some creaking iceberg, beneath whose summit lies the black depths of unseen and unknown ancestries. That we should not know our progenitors, beyond a certain point, is a statement of the bluntest rational necessity. And yet the fact remains; That when we imagine the chill hand of some faceless father clutching ours, and imagine the familiar blood whispering through unfamiliar arteries, then we are filled with a thrill of the uncanny. We do not like the feeling of being dependent on a chain that runs so deeply, or else one that is suspended so eerily from unascertainable hights.

It is in connection to this theme that I have presented here a largely unedited manuscript from my early days as a clinical psychotherapist. It shall no doubt be perplexing to the lay reader, as it has been both to myself and to many of my colleagues over the years.

The writing itself is taken from the clinical diary of a patient of mine, a physician of twenty years, who despite making great advances in his psychic wellbeing was never quite liberated from his psychotic tendencies, and his occasional mania. This excerpt was a recovered memory which came to be recollected by him some months into treatment. It is worth noting that its unearthing was followed by a period of intense perplexity whereafter he lived apart from his own family for an extended time.

Although one may at first scoff at its likeness to existing gothic conceits, its discovery yielded remarkable changes in my patient's personality. Indeed, it threw light on many aspects of his previous mania. For this man (the patient in question) had occasionally looked at his own son and seen the face of an unrecognised old fellow. Or looking at his own daughter playing upon the village green had seen a black-clad widow from an old family photograph pacing behind the laughing children.

Notably, Mr. [Redacted] suffered an attack of acute panic in hospital on the week before his first son was born. When questioned by the shocked nurse, who in a nervous fist still clutched a swinging stethoscope, only one stuttered answer was to be encountered in reply. It was the heart.

It was the sound of the heart.

As I say, I have presented the manuscript unrevised for clinical purposes.

Elias T. Joseph, 1930

The Spectacle

By Molly Kirk

'The mermaid embodies an imagined, more heightened evolved human condition that valorizes the necessary state of weakness,' – Lara Stevens and Denise Varney, *The Climate Siren*.

Selene hovers reluctantly at the dance floor's edge, just outside her pointy tent. She keenly watches as neat-looking server robots amble lazily up to her and her neighboring guests, offering up all manner of beverages, refreshments, and snacks. She has never seen such ostentatious riches before, and a pang of nausea washes briefly over her; despite the months of rehearsals to perfect her performance and overcome her paralyzing stage fright.

The darkened cavernous ballroom flickers in weak candlelight, creating an unnecessarily seductive effect. Pairs of shimmering dancing silhouettes flash past her in the shadows. Their dresses and suits shining silver, black, and gold as they twirl in time with the ghostly melody; each dancer reflecting a fractured moment, a crystalline film reel reflected within the chandeliers hanging above. The dancers look beautiful, serene. Years ago, she would have ogled at them in awe wishing she could be just like them. But her days of idle dreaming were long behind her and instead she rolls her eyes, repulsed by the scenery and the beautiful people filling it. After years spent as an outcast, living in squalor with those the upper-class had long since turned their backs on, this is her first time attending one of these events and her time to shine to prove herself worthy of looking at.

She sips nervously on expensive champagne, clutching the glass tightly in her gloved hands. She was surprised she had even been offered a drink in the first place, considering how she's one of tonight's amusements. Something for the wealthy patrons to gape at between dances; a welcome distraction from the state of the world outside. There was a reason this dance was being held in cool underground caverns. Probably just an oversight in the robot's programming.

'I guess the stupid machines can't even register the difference,' she mutters to herself, despite the clear oceans between her and *them*. Accompanied with a sharp pang in her chest, her mind drifts anxiously once more to the darkened waters of the big glass tank hidden inside of tent number five.

The shrouded hall is lined with somber black and white marquees to match the theme of this year's ball: Carnival.

'More like Freakshow', Selene angrily corrects, when talking to her fellow performers. They each offered reluctant grins in response, her words shaking them out of their individual reveries. Magnus gave a hearty laugh at her comment, his dazzling blue eyes offering her a supportive wink. His split-dyed black and white hair and matching suit, complimenting tonight's glitzy theme. They have all been specially selected by Magnus, a gentle upperclassman with an eye for theatrics. He treated them all like equals and even paid them for their work. Whilst they all have their own individual reasons for being here tonight the money is definitely a tempting incentive.

Within the first tent lies a veiled animatronic fortune teller, her metallic skin catching the light as she shuffles her deck of tarot cards. They liked to call her 'Astra', based off the few letters they could pick out from her model's registration code: 'AS345T68RA'. She's an older model, a relic of past human creation – built before synthetic skin was the norm – but people still trusted her enough to read their fortunes, as a machine would never lie, right?

The second contains a darkened room, illuminated by intricate white holograms: lions, elephants, dogs, doves, and bears, playing, and performing tricks, balancing on black and white balls, dancing on their hind legs, juggling, jumping through hoops. Despite being the products of a man-made machine, the animals seemed to have a life to them all of their own, their eyes containing the intelligence and adaptability of their once alive counterparts – now long extinct.

The third tent contains the funambulist, Amy. A timid, graceful creature, built like a petite black bird, with feathered wings sewn onto her costume to match. She can always be found perched atop a wire clutching her pretty pink parasol. The fourth tent contains Pixie, a limber, tattooed contortionist, every inch of her oily body covered in ink except her face.

'True beauty isn't skin deep.' She offered up as explanation one night, looking meaningfully at Selene as she said this.

As Pixie contorts herself, bending her body to unnatural angles, coiling up like a snake in the weakened lighting, her tattoos come alive. The dragon painted on her bald head seems to blink in a bemused manner as she performs, slithering down her body exploring its newfound terrain.

Last is Selene's tent, only containing her clear tank, like a giant goldfish bowl, tonight's final show.

An antique gothic grandfather clock strikes midnight somewhere within the shadows of the room, pulling Selene out of her mind. Announcing itself with twelve damning chimes that reverberate throughout her entire body. It's time. Slowly heading towards her tent, she can't shake the tight knots forming within her stomach. They threaten a hostile takeover, stealing the air from within her lungs, trying to convince her to hide, to run far away and not perform. She doubts any of these sheltered invitees have seen anything even close to her, how would they? If they had then who knows what would have happened to them, to her people.

A large group of wealthy patrons stand nearby giggling and whispering, the women dripping in diamonds and jewelry to the point where they themselves shine like automatons. She overhears snippets of their conversation:

'Why do the lowers even complain?'

'A warmer planet is better.'

'Who wants to be cold anyways?'

'Just because they can't afford to have air-conditioning...'

They all burst out laughing at this as Selene seethes, glaring right at them. They glance at her briefly before diverting their attention, quickly registering by her slanted posture and uneven stomping strides that she was far beneath them. Not worth their amusement. In time they'd understand just how wrong they were.

She hears loud squeals of delight from Pixie's tent, as the crowd of those curious enough to explore the tents has weaved their way from one side-show to the next. But she is the true showstopper.

Five years ago, Selene ran away from home, finding her way to Magnus and this curious troupe of misfits; surprised that circuses and freakshows even still existed outside of books – she supposed it ultimately made sense though. Human curiosity and the need for entertainment would never die, especially for those rich enough to still afford it.

Once safely inside her tent, shielded by black and white curtains, she exhales, hastily stripping off the constricting high-necked blue gown she is wearing. The human materials alien and itchy to her skin. With the assistance of Jesper, her adored stagehand and lover, she removes her gloves and heels as well. Next, she removes her contact lenses, changing her eye color from dark brown back to its original fluorescent green-yellow. Eventually she stands before him completely naked, stripped of her façade of normalcy, her makeup her only mask. Her heart hammers in her chest like a hummingbird trapped within her ribcage. Jesper stares at her ivory body in awe, admiring the scales that have coated almost every inch of her from below the neck since birth, the same pale blue green as a fresh bruise. She stretches, exposing deep indented slits on the side of her neck: her gills.

No one was sure how this happened exactly. Doctors suggested the high pollution and toxicity of the earth – perhaps a means of adapting to the rising sea-levels and constant flooding caused by climate change. She'd faced bullying her entire life. Hushed conversations amongst her parents, her mother's furrowed brow whenever she caught a glimpse of her gills and scaly skin, being repeatedly dragged kicking and screaming to see doctors just to be tested over and over again with no definitive results. She'd been forced to cover up her entire body just to go to school and fit in; so many tears spilt wishing she was *normal*. Jesper was the first to make her realize that she wasn't alone, that there are others like her out there too, other mutations: hybrids. Selene was drawn to Jesper more so than the others because of his confidence, he brought her stability and safety in an uncertain world. Jesper was the only one who could reach her in the midst of her panic attacks and he always instinctively knew what was going on inside her head before she did. He is safe and solid, too solid; abnormally strong with skin thick as stone and fully heat resistant. He accepts her, all the amusements accept her, just as she is.

No more hiding.

Enjoying this gentle moment with him away from everyone and everything she presses her body up to his, kissing him softly; he grounds her from the madness that is sure to follow. Her thoughts race, swirling in her mind and threatening to pull her under. He kisses her back passionately, cupping her face tenderly in his hands, treating this as though it were both the first and last time their lips would ever meet.

'Good luck Sel,' he whispers softly into her ear, lightly squeezing her webbed hands. She smiles at him, her face softening as she plays with his messy blonde hair and feels the tension within her ease, replaced by the feeling of his warmth. With his help she turns and climbs up the golden ladder at the side of the tank. Eventually standing alone on the platform above she looks down at the still pool beneath her, waiting, enticing her to jump in.

The guests slowly begin trickling into her tent, drawn in by Jesper's loud theatrical encouragements.

'Come and see the REAL spectacle now that you're all warmed up!' As the tent fills up, Selene finally steps out into the spotlight, her glinting scales giving her skin a blueish hue. A breathless quiet fills the space as people slowly take her in from far below, mouths open wide, all conversations caught forever in their own hushed throats. The shocked drawn-out silence is broken with a symphony of gasps and hushed whispers, whilst Magnus and the other amusements slowly shuffle in at the back - not wanting to miss a second of her special debut. They wave up at her. She gulps thinking about the rumors of her kind disappearing, being experimented on. She is doing this for them, she will not disappear under the radar like they did. These people would know her name.

She'd had a few close calls herself in the past where scientists would hear about her through all the doctors she saw as a child, from her fellow students who would catch a glimpse of her gills and report it to her teachers, and even occasionally her fellow amusements. But Magnus always protected her, sending them away with their tails between their legs, intimidating them with his authority alone. She remembered returning home one day to find her parents sitting somberly in the kitchen with two men in black suits.

Molly Kirk

Her mother had looked at her pleadingly, 'sit down sweetheart...' she had turned around, ran, and never looked back. Until now. She trembles on her podium, suddenly feeling very small. Even if there were scientists here tonight, she couldn't tell. The whole room could be full of them, it could be an ambush for all she knew. Her legs betray her, quivering both from the cold air against her scales and the ice within the audience's accusatory gazes. Staring at her bare feet she covers her body with webbed hands and lowers her head,, she is the naked object of all their scrutiny. She is nobody, the only special thing about her was her skin. Tears began brimming, collecting in the corners of her eyes, threating to spill out all over the place. She looks helplessly to Jesper, who stands near the ladder, always ready should she need him. He would never let anything happen to her. He nods once, intuitive recognition forming in his dark brown eyes before he begins climbing the ladder up to her.

This brought her back to their first ever rehearsal together, she'd had a huge panic attack. Her stage fright and fears of being captured stole the air right from her lungs. She fainted dead off the platform, and he dived right into the tank after her before carrying her limp body safely in his arms. She awoke as he gently covered her up with the shirt off his back, holding her and warming her with his body heat. She'd fallen in love with him right then and there; he was already in love with her at that point – he had been since he first saw her underwater, fully in her element. Although she could breathe fine underwater, she'd always felt deep down that he'd saved her life that day, a debt she hoped to repay in full.

When he reached her, he held her hand. 'It's okay honey, you're okay,' he murmured softly so that only she would hear. He tilted her chin up to look at him. 'You're a miracle. I know it, you know it. So, show them all.' At that particular moment she didn't feel like it, but she gritted her teeth and clenched her jaw, letting him guide her to the platform's edge hand-in-hand. Then, as though awakened from a trance she takes a step forward on her own, then another. Adrenalin pumps through her as she gains momentum as she raises her arms above her head before diving gracefully into the waters below.

The liquid cradles her, nurturing her and muffling the panicked shrieks around her as she elegantly breaks through the smooth surface, not making so much as a splash. The icy depths hydrate her scales, cradle her breasts, bring new life into her veins. Bubbles form around her as she takes her first baby breaths, in and out. She relaxes, closing her eyes, so happy to finally be back in the water; the tension, the hours spent on land slowly melting away with her body.

She lets herself sink deeper into the tank, ignoring the onlookers pressing their faces right up to the glass – not looking quite so beautiful now. She starts to feel herself dissolving, metamorphosizing, her body giving in to her new form as the depths continue to engulf her, flowing through her. She kicks both her legs out once more before pinning them together as she feels them changing, stretching luxuriously from two limbs into one. With a euphoric sigh, her body fully awakens. She shivers as her scales join down the middle, meeting to form a long glistening turquoise appendage crowned by soft pleated fins at the end that open up like a fan. Gliding through the water propelled forwards by her unfurling tail, she is no longer confined by the rules of gravity.

She is more graceful here than on land, twirling and moving with the water. She swims speedily towards the lip, the boundary, leaping back up into their world and taking a breath of fresh air, before somersaulting and diving back into submerged safety. She is divine like Venus, reborn and powerful. Unstoppable. Tendrils of her hair frame her face, seaweed brown, floating above her like a makeshift crown.

Defiantly she looks out once more to the daunting crowd beyond, unafraid, staring at each of them triumphantly as she swims past. She is forcing them to take all of her in, her untamed beauty; daring them to try taking her away to some lab whilst she holds them each accountable. She is worthy of living, existing. Her unique form, her scaled iridescent body providing a weathered map of time. She is tangible proof, a voice for all those like her, forced to adapt to a brutal world that these people would never know. Through their eyes she sees horror and disgust shift to teary-eyed astonishment. Her existence rekindling the childhood wonder and naivety everyone has surrounding mythical creatures in fairytales. Irrefutably confirming the possibility of their existence and the tragedy of their nature.

'She's a Mermaid!' One of them exclaims before the room erupts with applause and cheers as they look upon what their neglect had created.

Ouroboros

By Myles Riley

'You know, every time travel story — at least time travel to the past, if you can change the past — causes some paradox. You have to deal with it in some way. And so if you're a physicist or a logician, more to the point, you might say, "Well, that proves that time travel's impossible." But that hasn't stopped generations of filmmakers and fiction writers from creating stories where one way or another they get around the paradox.'
– James Gleick

The Dreamer

I've been having strange dreams recently. My doctor tells me it's the side effects of an overactive imagination, but I am less sure.

I would consider myself a dreamer certainly but in an aspirational sense. I've never been one to let my dreams come to fruition, certainly not in a metaphysical way as they do in the minds of most men.

Hallucinations... I hate the very thought. Maybe I'm not getting enough sleep. But the more ideas – the more dreams I seem to come up with, the more I see him.

He is but my shadow.

The reflection in the glass, he comes when I get my best dreams; my best ideas. Maybe the doctor's right; maybe I need more sleep.

Sleep perchance to dream... and I shall dream of rocket ships in an infinitesimal sky as I slip off to sleep again.

The Worker

I wake, I rise and I am off to work.

It was never something that I anticipated with abundant excitement before, but now every day I have off, I find myself longing for my next shift whenever I glance towards the limitless sky. There is of course, only one reason why.

I am twenty-seven; am of average height and I love the works of Joseph Haydn. I hate asparagus and I adore coffee.

She is twenty-eight; is of average height, and she is an avid enjoyer of Shakespeare. She dislikes snakes and ladders upon grounds of it being a simple simulation of chance without room for merit or strategy. She also hates asparagus as much as she adores coffee.

When we first met it wasn't exactly all fireworks and rainbows. You see:

I own a St. Bernard named... unoriginally, Bernard. He is

eight, is of average height and is a passionate proponent of pedigree dog food. He dislikes the works of Ivan Pavlov and he also adores coffee. Believe me it was not a pretty sight.

Well... there I was, standing in the line outside of one those trendy new coffee vans you see parked up on the street, waiting with an impatient Bernard, for an overwhelmed barista, as I refused to go to the Starbucks just across the way, being something of anti-corporatist.

Pretty ironic; considering I had just applied for a job with a private government grant sector.

Anyway, I got to the second place in the queue and Bernard, being the grumpy old man he is, had decided he had waited long enough.

Close enough to get the rich aroma of ground coffee beans up his nostrils, Bernard decided to perform blatant daylight robbery. Leaping up at the van's hatch, he sent the lady in front of me tumbling to the curb; hot beverage in hand.

She wasn't burnt. Some small miracle considering. In fact she was in fine condition from the fall, a sentiment that could not be extended to the real victim; the squashed brown takeaway cup, it's innards spilt across the pavement like blood. It's recyclable form crumpled and broken.

'What a waste.' I sighed.

'What a waste.' She chimed at the exact same time.

There was a brief moment as I looked to her before returning to stare solemnly at the crime scene. She turned to look back at me, hearing my mimicry.

And we shared a laugh.

By the time I'd eventually collected myself, she squinted at me, adjusting her glasses. 'Don't I know you?'

I stumbled for a moment in my ignorance. But she was already ahead, as I collected my thoughts, she had already solved the case.

'You applied for a job at my work!' She exclaimed. 'For some big theory you have. The higher ups seemed very impressed, you created quite the stir amongst the lab techies.'

'Wow I'm surprised you remember that.' It was a compliment sure, but not a false one. She must have been good at her job.

Maybe I should push for that position after all. Making the theoretical a reality has never been my strong suit, but, maybe it's time I stopped being just a dreamer.

The Spaceman

I'm not entirely sure what it is, but it's outside.

I don't think I was the first to wake up either.

The others are... missing.

In the night it sings;

a cold, dead frequency.

I'm too scared to look out of the bay window.

At best I would see the ghostly vacuum of space; an ode to the hopelessness of my situation.

At worst...

The ships computer is malformed.

I would have used the word malfunctioned.

However, the grotesque wraith that haunts the computer systems can no longer be considered artificial intelligence.

At first I had hoped this was merely a case of machine sentience. Tales of rogue AI were not uncommon back on Earth. However I believe the rest of the crew met a far worse fate than machine slaughter.

Whilst my first glimpse at the decomposing sludge did terrify, even after I witness the remnant of a human eye staring back at me, its fleshy form does little to distract from what awaits out there. I can only assume the computer's corruption a small part of whatever grand machination this external entity has designed.

I am in two minds about whether to offer myself to the main computers collection.

Whilst death doth appear appealing, I doubt it would do much to rectify my situation.

Whatever awaits out there creates reality's rule book… there is no guarantee it abides by it.

The Shadow

We are the same.

I observe myself in him as he moves across the walkway. Passing by the coffee shop window where I observe his routines, procrastinating on the taking of a life…

No job, no pets, no significant other; no one to miss him. A solitary state, as I once knew.

Empathy. Maybe that's why I feel bad for him, but it cannot be denied; he is perfect for my means.

My trigger finger itches, I've come this far, I mustn't back down at the final hurdle, till red runs the clocks back; the river Styx in reverse.

The Dreamer

It's too hot.

I think people would call this a slump. It's not as if I didn't choose this though. The interview went well and the pay is insane. Private funding, huge budget, practically my own boss...

Hah, right.

But still, why sit here and demerit it? Tis undoubtedly my best idea yet; my biggest dream, but still I find no drive to become a worker, no desire to do more.

And as usual he is nearby; my shadow. Not surprising considering the scale of this dream of mine. But I'm sure I could make him out in the crowd earlier; a person not simply a reflection so familiar, so tangible. That must be giving me this uneasy feeling, not the interview.

Maybe I need more sleep. Probably shouldn't have ordered more caffeine then.

Ow, my tongue... still too hot.

The Worker

I love her. Of that I have no doubt. She inspires me; through the work we do together, she drives me forward. The dream is alive in her. But it matters little to me, not in comparison to how I feel.

If I were an indolent artist, she would be a muse. But if I were not a physicist, would she take the time to choose?

She is passionate about the work and, I suppose, in a way, I am the work. But if the work belonged to another, would her passion be of equal measure?

'You certainly look engaged,' she interrupts my daydreaming.

'Thanks.' I rub my eyes. I'll admit, not being such a dreamer has me getting less sleep.

'Don't let Bernard know, but they restocked the beans in the machine.' She whispers in faux slyness as she places her contraband; coffee in front of me.

It's a peace offering.

We argued during the meeting with the ethics board, who are surprisingly clinical with ethics. It was determined quite quickly one condition made the proposition of 'proof' quite 'lawful'.

Apparently entities of plane A (ourselves) had political immunity to the laws of plane B, being such that we have no citizenship and by that nature legal existence. Thus the matter was not an issue as far as ethical conduct was concerned. One cannot commit a crime if one does not exist. What an impressive loophole in morality for something so malevolent.

I had been secretly opposed to the whole thing, but she was far more enthusiastic about the work than I. And this was my idea after all. As such I felt the only thing I could do was offer myself as martyr.

That, interestingly, had been where we had fallen out.

I could almost mistake it for concern.

As if the whole mission were not fraught with risk enough anyway.

I look to the coffee, and back to her. She has accepted my decision to bear the burden, although she is still clearly opposed.

If I were to die - would it truly upset her so?

The Spaceman

The computer appears mindless, I am certain it poses little threat as its patterns are regular and unchanging. Clearly my former crewmates eventually gave in to the desperate thoughts now teeming in the back of my mind and offered themselves to it... hopeful, desperate lambs.

By carefully avoiding it I have managed to learn much about my situation. Yet what I have learnt confuses me further.

The ship is not adrift but stationary in time betwixt spaces, between all that is known. I believe that the real threat is whatever awaits me outside. That which plucked us from our backwards passage through the three dimensions.

And while it is not alive.

It is conscious.

I do not know how this is possible.

I believe it is portraying an emotion we might ascribe as... anger.

I believe our attempted trip has angered it.

And while I know we are not travelling through time with the rest of the universe, we appear to be prescribed our own time here. Then again how would I know, I couldn't possibly perceive otherwise.

It sings when I feel I must sleep.

It is a cold song, unwelcoming.

And I can only hope; the fever dream of my madness. Could this really be reality?

The Shadow

To paradox or not to paradox that is the question.

Whether tis nobler in the mind to suffer the uncertainty and fear of surrender or to risk taking up action against one's own existence. And by opposing end them. To die - to sleep.

To sleep - perchance to live. For in that sleep of death what chances may come when we have shuffled off this mortal coil and onto another. Must give us pause – there's the respect that makes calamity of so long life.

For who would bear the whips and scorns of time – when time could be defied?

Myles Riley

Should I draw near? Should I play Redcrosse, slay my demons, approach Kafka's castle? Is the right ours to defy nature so or is this hubris most folly. Hark I come, I'll draw back for now. For time is something I have plenty of. And now, has plenty... of me.

*

The Dreamer

He's here.

Why is it we rail against the obvious with blind hope? That the inevitable always seems to come as a surprise?

That stories could possibly shock us at their demise?

It the normality of it I suppose. Today was a day like any other.

I woke late, with nothing to stir my dreams but this living, waking one I spurn.

For private in my chamber would I pen myself,

Shut the windows and lock fair daylight out,

And make for myself an artificial night. Nothing good ever came of light.

Coffee is what keeps me dreaming, lets me walk further in this waking one. Though, the dream of life is a dull drab record, looped upon repeat.

I walk to the coffee van; artisan. I've settled on one now, one that feels right. By two o'clock I usually have it in hand, ready to walk back again – the exercise of the day – the excuse being fresh air.

My usual route takes me past this canine rescue shelter that had never really stood out to me before. But today, as I walk back, coffee in hand, I notice the window was ajar. Unusual: Perhaps the dogs were also getting some fresh air.

As I pass, this great lump; a St. Bernard leaps up at the window, barking like mad. I stagger a few paces off the curb in shock. Yet when I look into this hound's eyes, I feel a connection, a familiarity: A life I hadn't lived, stretched out like twine; an elastic lifetime.

His eyes were on my cup, the smell of coffee must have roused him so; no wonder I feel a connection, what a strange mutt.

I want to linger, but as I draw close I feel his presence; the laboured breath of the wolf on the hunt.

This new connection a catalyst.

And me, the prey animal, heightened sense, eyes all about.

He is at my side. Is that the glint of metal emerging from his pocket? He reaches out.

I run.

But you cannot outrun the monsters we make for ourselves; the parts of us we must learn to live with, or else have them conquer us. Consume us.

Corner us.

He stands before me. Trapped down an alley; nowhere left to run. Stuck between my mirror and a hard place.

Legacies cannot be left of dreams alone.

Myles Riley

The Worker

The final checks are complete, all the simulations run. We are ready to begin the mission, the work is almost complete.

I stand in the cockpit, taking in the controls in front of me. I find my seat and from behind I hear her soft laugh.

'Did you go to the bathroom before we set off?'

I eye her up sarcastically. I'm surprised she seems so relaxed, although she was always more confident in our calculations than I.

'Better strap yourself in soon, lest you want to be catapulted into a parallel universe without your seatbelt on.'

She laughs at that. The ships computer whirs past us and plugs itself into the mainframe console; we're out of time. I sit myself across from her as the crew assembles around us.

But my eyes are all on her, as the countdown whisks the time away; I reach reflexively for her hand.

9...8...7...

She returns my gaze and for a moment all is clear as the engines ignite.

6...5...4...

And with a deep breath as the stabiliser canisters drip away: 'Will you marry me?'

3...2...1...

Blast off.

The Spaceman

I think it's on board with me now, I would say it was tired of waiting for me but I think I know what it is now. And, if I'm right, how could it possibly have a concept of boredom.

It's reaching out to my other senses now not just aural. It shows me things...hallucinations, I think, that I believe are twisted conceptions of itself.

I am speaking to the Constant: c.

How foolish, how silly.

c does not reply to me.

How foolish, how silly.

I only pray that no others attempt to defy time as we have.

How foolish, how silly.

What I wouldn't give for a coffee.

But there is hope.

Every waking minute since I gained consciousness on this plane I have been searching for answers. Not because I care to know the hopelessness of my situation, but because answers are a trade she dealt in well.

Her pod was empty, and I cannot get close enough to the mainframe to identify the... parts.

So, all I have left are questions and if anyone could hope to understand the conscious of a Constant, it would be her. Asking the same questions she did may be the only way I have left to trace her in an other-wise intangible universe.

Following her intellectual footsteps has led me to believe that I am a memory, a snapshot, a recording.

I think our trip was successful.

We are the imprint left between the universes.

Somewhere my crew and I are safe: She is safe.

And I am the version left here to suffer.

This is the clarity my shipmates came to and while I know it forlorn,

The temptation of possibility is too great.

I let the computer find me.

May my disassembly be quick.

I pray this proves punishment enough.

Though I have no gods left to pray to;

Just judge, jury and executioner -

The law of light speed itself.

The Shadow

It is time; I have concluded that I must take the final test. Whether or not my theory is correct, I will conclude today. The crew wait on me.

If I die then I live.

If I live then I will never have lived at all.

And if I'm wrong and I never exist at all, then what's the harm in dying?

***

I think I know. From the way I'm looking at myself I've already guessed my fate. I tremble in the alleyway, stare back at myself as I approach. Unlike me, I have not accepted this. Fear is all I can read in my eyes, probably doubled by my uncertainty. Today I die... or the universe dies with me.

And then I can live.

I take the knife from my pocket. It will be enough. I must prove my hypothesis correct. It's just a shame I have to kill myself to do it.

One small death for man.

One giant leap for mankind.

Everything Ends

By Oliver D. Kleinschmidt

Wrapped in layers of winter clothing a young girl shivers against the cold. She makes for a slight figure cut against the unforgiving steel of a doorway as she rubs her gloved hands together. Wild winds steal away the steady puffs of breath and she presses into a corner. She stamps her feet and pulls off one glove to better access the inside of the keypad before her. Her fingers shake, the tips blue, as she uses a pair of minute pliers to pull a thin copper wire from the door's keypad and presses it to another. Sparks spit fitfully yet the frozen door offers no relief from the raging blizzard sweeping the city ruins.

Her heart hammers behind her ribcage. She drops a length of copper and loses it in the snow gathering around her boots. Beneath the winds there is another sound; footsteps, falling rubble? The hunter?

She pulls another wire from her pocket and presses the two

wires together. She squeals with delight as they spark and spit. There comes a grinding of gears and a rusted screech as the door slides open. Frost crunches beneath the child's boots as she rushes inside and furiously rubs her hands together. The passage is dim. She turns on her head torch as lights ahead fail to function and feebly flicker before giving up and dying into a glimmer of yellow light. From a speaker, a distorted female voice crackles into life.

'Hello. Welcome to the BioLife Research Facility, "Forging a brighter future, for you".'

The small child timidly pulls back the fur-lined hood of her thick coat.

'Hello Felicity!' The girl's voice echoes around the room. She cannot be any older than nine, perhaps on the cusp of ten. Her hair is a carefully constructed braid and her dimpled cheeks are spotted with freckles. Her eyes gleam with icy sharpness.

'Welcome back Alice. Are you alone again?'

Through the open door the wind screams. Alice's gaze drifts to the outside. Ice falls harder and the surrounding skyscrapers are barely visible through the blinding shield of white snow. From the opposite street, a shadow steps forward.

'No.' she says calmly. Alice's headtorch cuts through the darkness; light falls across walls covered in crawling patterns of frost. Wires hang low from dislodged panels in the ceiling leaving trailing vines of electrical wiring. Glass cracks beneath her foot as she cuts through a workspace that might have once been a laboratory. 'Alice. It has been forty-two days since your last visit to this facility. In the subsequent time it has suffered catastrophic damage.'

The girl shoulders her rucksack and presses onward into the heart of the building. 'Are you okay Felicity? Your CPU is still running, right?'

'My main CPU housing unit remains undamaged and continues to function.'

With stanch determination Alice picks up her pace and gasps as she is struck by penetrating rays of light streaming from somewhere up high. Her eyes take a moment to adjust to the intrusive brightness before she can bring herself to gaze up.

She stands on a balcony at one end of a large atrium. Sunlight streams through the gaping maw of the hole in the ceiling where an ornate skylight once provided ample streams of light to this wide, open space. Jagged bars of steel and iron spear the ground below in a twisted display of glinting metal. Shards of glass glint in the overhead sunlight. Alice takes a step back from the edge.

Across the chasm of the atrium is a concrete pillar that must've fallen through from further up. Patches of ice cling to its cracked form. One end has crashed into the balcony before her and the other balances precariously across the chasm of the atrium so that the entire thing lay on an awkward horizontal axis. A few odd steel cables wrap around it, straining to hold up the concrete monstrosity. Alice worries her lower lip; there is no other way across. Her nails press into her palms, leaving deep, red impressions. Shaking, she grabs the pillar and hoists herself up onto its craggy surface; her knees wobble and the ground only seems further away than it did before. The distance to the opposite balcony cannot be far; no more than ten, maybe twelve meters? But she still struggles with every step forward. She's clever for her age, she knows about what happens to little girls who are not careful.

Her foot slips on a patch of ice and her stomach lurches as she falls. She claws at the pillar, her arms flailing, and catches hold of a jagged rock. Pain slices through her palm but she clings on; her nimble fingers finding purchase. Blood flows, bright and colourful against the white, powdery snow. Alice crawls the rest of the way on her hands and knees and when she finally reaches the other side she collapses and wipes the thick sheen of sweat from her brow.

Blood drips onto the floor. Somewhere else, glass cracks beneath a boot. Alice jumps up and casts a worried glance behind her. Her eyes dart around the corridor, the atrium, the pillar. There is no one there.

'Are you feeling well? Your heartrate has been elevated.' Felicity asks. Alice wraps a length of bandages around her palm. The wound doesn't bleed as much anymore but every time she brushes the ragged edges she is shocked by an electric jolt of pain. 'Felicity? Can you feel pain?'

There comes a long pause as Alice traverses the darkened corridors and vacant offices. 'I am a machine and therefore cannot be harmed.'

'Do you ever get scared?'

'No.' The reply comes quick. As she turns a corner her light sputters out. Alice rips the headtorch off and frantically fumbles with it in the dark. She shakes it, tries to pull open the battery compartment. Yet despite her best efforts she remains in darkness with only a few shapes noticeable through the gloom.

She crawls forward, feeling her way through the dark. Her breathing is sharp and quick. She's read stories of the things that hide in the dark to steal away lonely children.

When Felicity speaks Alice almost cries out of sheer relief. 'Alice. Are you afraid?'

Alice smiles sheepishly as her torch finally flickers and brightens the corridor. 'Not anymore.'

After clambering over a series of fallen filing cabinets thrown down in the middle of the corridor Felicity's voice crackles through the speaker above her head. 'Another person has entered the facility.'

There is a hollow silence that is broken by Felicity's calm, cold voice. 'It appears your companion is not willing to communicate with me.'

Alice bites her lip and rubs at her eyes. 'It's not my companion.'

'If it is not your companion then what are they? They appear to be human.'

Alice plays with a curl of hair, twisting it between her thumb and forefinger. 'It's a monster.'

It is hard for Alice to ignore the cold shiver that dances its way along her spine. How long had the hunter been following her? Nonetheless, Alice has a task, something she has to do. Undaunted, Alice continues to crawl into the depths of the facility. Frost no longer covered everything as the blizzards had yet to penetrate this deep into the heart of the complex.

Eventually her way is lit by the florescent glow of the overhead lighting as it flickers into life with her progress.

Everything Ends

'Thank you, Felicity.' Alice quietly whispers.

She follows the lights as each one dimly points the way to her objective. Finally, Alice rises to her feet, her hands and knees bruised and worn, her back aching from the weight of her rucksack. She clenches her fist as the cut on her right hand throbs insistently. She stands before a room enclosed by walls of thick glass. A faded metal sign reads in a dead language: *Central Data Server*. Simon had taught her to read English since much of the food they scavenged had labels written in it. However, as far as she knew there was no other people left in the city who could still read.

Inside, stacked towers of servers reach from floor to ceiling. Most are dark and silent. Two still continue to glow and there remains a faint hum of electric energy as these two data banks work tirelessly to keep Felicity alive. Cables run through the ceiling from both servers and into the central console. Alice recognises all this, and she knows what she must do.

'Felicity, do you know where I can find your CPU?'

'Of course, it is located in the central terminal, rack four, row nine. Would you like assistance in finding it?'

Alice doesn't know if the cameras are still working but she shakes her head. 'No thank you. Simon showed me where to find it the last time we were here.'

'And how is Simon?'

Alice hesitates before answering, 'he's just sleeping.'

She finds the main control unit with little difficultly. It is a larger structure with a network of interconnected wires and tubes reaching from the ceiling and connecting into the top of the pillar. An electric hum emanates in a powerful signal that radiates from the heart of the machine in a constant rhythmic pulse that beats with a consistent pattern.

Alice rubs her hands together and retrieves her toolkit from the depths of her rucksack. It takes her a few minutes to find the screws and remove the front panel. Inside she carefully reaches in and wraps her fist around the CPU. Clasped in her palm it feels small and insignificant. It thrums gently with power.

'I'm sorry Felicity.' After checking the CPU is there Alice takes the containment capsule from her rucksack and opens it. As she prepares it to receive the CPU she looks up at the pulse of the machine. 'Felicity?'

'Yes.'

'Will you die?'

Seconds tick past, filling the silence with nought but machine noise.

'Machines are not alive Alice. Therefore, I cannot die.'

'But what about shutting down? Machines can stop working right?'

'Alice. Everything has to end eventually.'

Sighing, Alice finishes preparing the capsule and reaches into the heart of Felicity. 'You can't feel pain, right?'

'No'.

Alice's fingers grip the CPU and pull. It releases with a little *click* and the blinking lights die out in an instant. No gasping breath, no drawn-out final words. Just pure silence and the steady crunch of boots as Alice leaves the server room behind with the CPU stashed away in her rucksack. Finally, she has what she came for and can return to Simon.

There's a light up ahead. The burning orange of flickering fire casts long shadows on the wall. The silhouette of a tall, lithe figure rounds the corner up ahead and raises the makeshift torch high. Alice freezes before scurrying into an alcove.

The firelight reflects in the hunter's pupils as they approach. Her clothes hang around her in trailing tatters of woollen garments scavenged from her victims, her hair hangs long and lank, permanently damp with snowflakes clinging to her pale skin. The only thing Alice is certain of is that the hunter is a human woman.

Across her back is a bow and quiver, and in her free hand she holds aloft a serrated dagger, its edges sharpened with malice. She sniffs the air and her smile splits her face like a crescent moon. She extinguishes her torch and plunges the corridor into darkness. Alice hasn't got much time.

Slowly she reaches out and takes a piece of debris. It's a small piece of wall plaster but it should be enough. The hunter's footsteps grow louder and there is the scraping of wood on wood as she nocks an arrow. It is now or never for Alice.

In one mighty movement Alice catapults the piece of plaster across the corridor to the other side. There's a cracking sound as it impacts on the far floor. The hunter curses and spins on her heels, racing down the corridor and away from Alice.

With the utmost surety Alice leaps to her feet and sprints

as fast as she can down the passage and away to the atrium. There is no hesitation in her eyes as she clambers onto the pillar and half climbs, half slips across the beam. All she has to do is get outside and she can lose the hunter in the storm. Ahead she can see the balcony, its' not far; five meters, four meters...

A lance of pain impales her thigh, and she screams out in anguish. Slipping she catches a piece of rebar and hangs on for dear life. The pain is unbearable and carves into her thigh like a hot knife. When she moves, she feels muscle contract around the arrow shaft and the metal tip graze against the bone of her femur. Far below, those metal shards of debris suddenly seem much closer.

Still, Alice has come too far. She hauls herself up and onto the pillar. Behind her the hunter stands, bow in hand, already nocking another arrow. Beneath them the icy bridge cracks and the pillar groans due to their combined weight. The hunter takes aim and steps forward. Alice squeezes her eyes shut.

There's a yell as the hunter slips. The hunter steadies her footing and digs her heels into the bridge. Alice feels the cold of the ice and concrete beneath her fingers and can already feel the tears on her cheeks freeze.

Without hesitation she pulls out her water canteen and begins pouring; emptying it onto the pillar. She shakes the last droplets from the container and drags herself backwards as the hunter advances, another arrow already drawn. Alice watches the hunter step onto the rapidly freezing patch of water.

The hunter slips, Alice smiles. She's won. The hunter

takes another step, her foot goes out from under her and she topples. Alice can see her eyes in that moment, wide with fear and pleading desperately. Her hand claws through the air and Alice follows her as she hits the ground with a slicing crunch.

A steel rod has driven itself through the stomach of the hunter. Blood pours in thin streams from her body and spreads in a small pool. Her chest hitches as she wheezes and gasps, specks of crimson stain her lips and she coughs as one hand grips the debris embedded in her midsection.

Alice stays until the hunter's gasps and groans bubble in her mouth before finally gurgling to a stop.

Perched upon the pillar, Alice continues to watch as the hunter's eyes turn glassy. She is gone, just like Felicity and almost like herself. She tries to put pressure on her leg but tendrils of pain force her to recoil. She remembers what Simon had taught her about the need for pressure.

Simon.

Alice nearly bites through her tongue when she pulled the arrow from her leg and dresses the wound. Before she makes for the exit she looks down at the pale face of the hunter. Glassy eyes stare aimlessly at the distant sky beyond the surrounding ruins.

'Sorry.'

***

It takes her two days to get back to the hideout as she drags herself across the city. By now the snowstorm has subsided from a raging blizzard to a gusting wind that brings with it the occasional drifting snowflake to rest on her head.

The hideout entrance is no more than a hatch hidden behind an alley, but she finds it with no problem. Her arms ache as she lifts the hatch and climbs down the ladder but she can only breathe a sigh of relief to be home. She turns on a switch and a collection of overhead christmas-lights illuminate the basement.

In a corner sits an occupied armchair that they'd taken from the furniture store down the street. In it sits a polished humanoid android slumped forward. The identification bar on its chest reads S1M0-N/57. Its typically featureless face has a large grin and smiling eyes drawn on in crayon.

Alice limps up to it and taps its head for access to its Information Processing Unit. She inserts the retrieved CPU and takes a hesitant step backwards. There is an electric whirring and the humanoid shudders before it raises its head. 'Hello Alice, I see you successfully found me a new processing unit.' It places a hand to its chest, 'thank you'.

Alice runs forward and wraps her arms around the warming metal of its frame. 'I'm happy you're back Simon.'

'Alice, it is almost time for your dinner. What would you like to eat?'

She sinks into the armchair and starts to unwrap her bandages. 'I'm not hungry.'

'Are you feeling well? Lack of appetite can be an indicator of poor health.'

She takes her time to unwrap the bandage around her leg; the wound continues to irritate her and throbs and itches. It almost is enough to distract from the pain in her hand, although that injury has finally started to heal. Simon walks over and hands her one of the medical kits they took from the hospital ruins. 'I missed you.'

'Thank you, Alice.' Suddenly Simon stands straight, and an insistent whine emanates from his voice box. 'Alice, I must inform you that I have only 750 days left of operating power before I shut down completely. I can advise you where to find a new power cell to —'

Alice rushed forward and once more wraps her arms around him; she squeezes him in a tight hug and presses her face against his midsection.

'That's okay. Everything has to end, eventually.'

Thank you for reading, Stranger.

Contributors

Alexander Masters is an experimental fiction writer who was selected as a winner for the Cotswold Creative Competition in 2020. He is most interested in exploring multiple genres, especially sci-fi and fantasy, and he is currently studying English Literature and Creative Writing at the University of Birmingham.

Amy Rafferty is a third-year student studying English Literature at the University of Exeter's Penryn campus. She has just completed her Creative Writing dissertation, inspired by the short stories of Anton Chekhov, Kevin Brockmeier and Kate Chopin. One of Amy's short stories *Leaving the Void* has been selected for the MoLS issue of *Riptide*.

Blakeney Clark is a recent graduate from the University of Exeter where she studied English Literature whilst writing for the university's creative writing journal, *Enigma*. Since graduating, she has continued to share her love of stories through organising the Linton Book Festival.

Born and raised in Ukraine **Nataliia Chubenko** moved to the UK to pursue her passion for literature at the University of Birmingham. She is an English and Creative Writing student and an aspiring writer making her first steps in the literary field with her debut short story in this collection.

James Albin is a thinker and writer from Dorset, England. Immersed in all questions of the supernormal and strange, he strives to present thoughts, images, and ideas from outside the realm of everyday experience. In 2022 he graduated from the University of Oxford with a degree in Theology. His current primary inspirations are the short stories of Arthur Machen, and the whole wealth of world folklore.

Jasmine Collins is an emerging writer from the Midlands. She writes prose, spoken word pieces and plays that she hopes help to educate, inspire and challenge societal norms. Her recent work includes Kickback Theatre's 'OUT OF YOUR

Contributors

MIND' and she is currently undertaking a Creative Writing MA at the University of Birmingham.

Molly Kirk is an emerging writer currently pursuing a Publishing MA at the University of Exeter where she also received her Law LLB. She is a contributing writer to the student literature journal *Enigma* and has been working as their Poetry Editor since 2022.

Myles Riley is a recent English BA graduate from Exeter University with a passion to update the mediums we consider normal in creative writing endeavours. Myles specialises in incorporating multiple forms of media into his creative writing process as well as exploring new ways to write. Therefore, he founded Tanks and Tankards – An Indie TTRPG company dedicated to retelling and creating WWII stories via a simulative experience.

Oliver D. Kleinschmidt is an emerging writer from the South-West with a History BA and currently pursuing a Publishing MA at the University of Exeter. He has worked on the publication of *Riptide vol. 15 Breath* as part of the author liaison team and digital marketing team and has written for the newspaper *Exeposé*. Currently he is working on his next project titled *Children of Rust*.

Roberto Oduor is a bookworm and basketball fan from Kenya with drive for storytelling led him to give a TEDx talk on his 'Road to Writing,' when he was 12 and write *Swish*: his first published story. He is currently working on his second book. Check out his blog at blogbybobomuga.blogspot.com.

Will Moran (they/he) is an MA Publishing student at the University of Exeter. They are a UniSlam 2022 winner and a commended poet for The Magdalena Young Poets Prize. Their work has appeared in *The Madrigal Press, Celestite, Fifth Wheel Press* and others. They can be found on Twitter@ willrmoran.

www.ingramcontent.com/pod-product-compliance
Lightning Source LLC
Chambersburg PA
CBHW031121080526
44587CB00011B/1067